THE
RISE OF
CAPITALISM

MAIN THEMES IN EUROPEAN HISTORY

Bruce Mazlish, General Editor

THE RISE

OF

CAPITALISM

Edited by

Dᴀᴠɪᴅ S. Lᴀɴᴅᴇs

Harvard University

THE MACMILLAN COMPANY, NEW YORK
COLLIER-MACMILLAN LIMITED, LONDON

First Printing

Library of Congress catalog card number: 66–17385

THE MACMILLAN COMPANY, NEW YORK
COLLIER-MACMILLAN CANADA, LTD., TORONTO, ONTARIO

PRINTED IN THE UNITED STATES OF AMERICA

FOREWORD

History, we are frequently told, is a seamless web. However, by isolating and studying the strands that compose the tapestry of man's past, we are able to discern the pattern, or patterns, of which it is comprised. Such an effort does not preclude a grasp of the warp and woof, and the interplay of the strands; rather, it eventually demands and facilitates such a comprehension. It is with this in mind that the individual volumes of the MAIN THEMES series have been conceived.

The student will discover, for example, that the population changes discussed in one volume relate to the changes in technology traced in another volume; that both changes are affected by, and affect in turn, religious and intellectual developments; and that all of these changes and many more ramify into a complicated historical network through all the volumes. In following through this complex interrelationship of the parts, the student recreates for himself the unity of history.

Each volume achieves its purpose, and its appeal to a general audience, by presenting the best articles by experts in the field of history and allied disciplines. In a number of cases, the articles have been translated into English for the first time. The individual volume editor has linked these contributions into an integrated account of his theme, and supplied a selected bibliography by means of footnotes for the student who wishes to pursue the topic further. The introduction is an original treatment of the problems in the particular field. It provides continuity and background for the articles, points out gaps in the existing literature, offers new interpretations, and suggests further research.

The volumes in this series afford the student of history an unusual opportunity to explore subjects either not treated, or touched upon lightly in a survey text. Some examples are population—the dramatis personae of history; war—the way of waging peace by other means; the rise of technology and science in relation to society; the role of religious and cultural ideas and institutions; the continuous ebb and flow of exploration and colonialism; and the political and economic works contrived by modern man. Holding fast to these Ariadne threads, the student penetrates the fascinating labyrinth of history.

BRUCE MAZLISH
General Editor

CONTENTS

INTRODUCTION

For the purposes of this volume, capitalism is defined as an economic order in a specific historical context. On the one hand, it is an economic system based preponderantly on the private ownership and use of capital for the production and exchange of goods and services with the aim of earning a profit. In this sense, the system is theoretically not limited by time and place and can be described and analyzed in the abstract language of the economist.

On the other hand, capitalism is a determinate historical phenomenon, an institutional order that has developed in the West (that is, Europe and its transoceanic offshoots) and spread in the past century to at least one non-Western society, Japan. In Europe, it is a successor to an earlier institutional order known variously as feudalism, manorialism, or feudalism-manorialism, or sometimes simply as "the medieval economy." The salient characteristic of this economy was the organization of production and consumption in estates or village communities which aimed at something close to self-sufficiency.[1] In fact, few estates were capable of working and living in complete isolation. Certain necessities—salt, tar for the livestock (a remedy for skin disease), iron for tools—usually had to come from outside. And fewer still wanted to live in isolation. There was, throughout the Middle Ages, a trade, however thready and haphazard, in spices, *objets d'art,* bric-a-brac, fine cloth, and even so bulky a commodity as wine.

The transition from this economy of self-sufficiency to one of exchange for profit took place over centuries. It began with the cessation of foreign invasion and incursion (Normans, Magyars, Saracens) in the tenth century and the restoration of active and regular commercial intercourse over short and long distances. This expansion of trade

---

[1] The estate and village community were two aspects of rural organization. The estate was essentially a production-property unit, combining a lord (who might be a person or collectivity), a demarcated area of land (not necessarily contiguous), and a body of workers (peasants) with varying bundles of obligations (labor, services, goods, money). The primary function of the estate was to sustain the lord and his household or contribute thereto. The village was a unit of settlement and derived originally from kinship or social ties and from the need for mutual assistance and protection. It far antedates the estate historically; indeed its origins are lost in prehistoric time. In the Middle Ages, a given estate might coincide territorially with a given village and its lands; it might include a number of villages; or it might consist of only part of a village.

brought with it the growth of urban centers, old and new, and an ever higher degree of occupational specialization. Skilled artisans congregated in the towns and cities, which became nodes of manufacture as well as commerce; estates that had once supplied their own industrial needs now concentrated on the cultivation of cash crops and obtained their goods and services in the marketplace. The whole process was self-sustaining and self-reinforcing. Division of labor along lines of comparative advantage yielded important gains in productivity and income, with concomitant savings in cost and increases in effective demand; while the improvements in quality that went with the development of specialized skills encouraged consumers to substitute market products for their homemade equivalents.[2]

This outline is the essence of what the economist would call a model of economic change. But such a model is only a part of the story. It is too impersonal, too mechanistic. As the great Belgian historian Henri Pirenne pointed out in a classic article on "the stages of capitalism," the expansion of European commerce and industry owed much to the energy, opportunism, and inventiveness of a new breed of men, wanderers on the routes of trade or city dwellers, in either case living away from the soil and outside the traditional agrarian society.[3] To be sure, the separation was rarely so absolute as Pirenne implied. Medieval towns merged into the countryside; even massive walls did not always serve to separate streets and fields. Furthermore, the commercialization of agriculture offered enterprising peasants a chance to branch out into trade and live in both worlds; and this duality remained into the nineteenth century a major channel of recruitment of business talent. Yet commerce and industry were jealous masters, and where they throve, the fields gave way to houses, and peasants abandoned agriculture for more lucrative pursuits.

In any event, it was this new breed, urban and rural, entrepreneurs and artisans, who gave this surge of growth its dynamism and made it a change of kind as well as degree. This transitional period (roughly the tenth to the fourteenth century) was one of experiment and innovation. In manufacturing the most impressive advance was perhaps the application of water power to the fulling hammers (to give body

    [2] An excellent brief discussion of these changes in one area of Europe is found in Georges Duby and Robert Mandrou, *A History of French Civilization from the Year 1000 to the Present* (New York, 1964), pp. 5–12, 59–76. The best comprehensive discussion remains the *Cambridge Economic History of Europe,* Vol. II: *Trade and Industry in the Middle Ages* (Cambridge, 1952).

    [3] Henri Pirenne, "The Stages in the Social History of Capitalism," *American Historical Review,* **XIX** (1913–1914), pp. 494–515.

to the cloth) and the forge, because the substitution of inanimate for animate sources of power is the critical criterion and condition of a modern industrial technology. In trade, a cluster of fundamental changes in the organization of enterprise and the techniques of exchange constituted what one scholar has described as the "Commercial Revolution." [4] Partnership arrangements were devised to meet the needs of the single venture or the continuing operation, to marry money and management, to join the members of a single family or a group of strangers. New commercial instruments were invented or old ones revived. The most important was the bill of exchange, originally a promissory note, eventually an acknowledgement of a debt payable at a later date in another place. This document accomplished two purposes: it facilitated the extension of credit in spite of usury laws; and it made it possible to make payments over a distance by remittance of paper rather than coin and bullion.

Pirenne was writing about the pioneers of economic change. Yet to understand the expansion of the capitalist sector, one must also take into account the overall growth in population, which perhaps doubled from the eleventh to the fourteenth century. There had been nothing comparable probably since the Neolithic age, and this surge was not to be duplicated or surpassed until the demographic explosion of the eighteenth and nineteenth centuries.

More people required more food and manufactures. Population soon exceeded the resources of the older settled areas, and men began to move in search of new land. Within the boundaries of medieval Europe, land-hungry peasants created an internal frontier: woods were cleared, marshes drained, polders reclaimed from the sea; while on the periphery, external frontiers were opened: east of the Elbe, south of the Pyrenees, eastward in the Mediterranean.

Colonization and conquest contributed mightily to the transformation of the European economy and society. On the one hand, movement was a solvent of the old order. The settlers of new land generally secured for themselves more favorable conditions of tenure and greater personal freedom than they had known in their old homes; and these advantages conduced in their turn to higher productivity and a more sensitive response to market opportunity. Even those who did not move

---

[4] See Raymond de Roover, "The Commercial Revolution of the Thirteenth Century," *Bulletin of the Business Historical Society*, **XVI** (1942), pp. 34–39; reprinted in Frederic C. Lane and J. C. Riemersma (eds.), *Enterprise and Secular Change: Readings in Economic History* (Homewood, Ill., 1953), pp. 80–85.

benefited; for their masters had to take account, in dealing with them, of the temptations of the world that was opening up outside the estate.

On the other hand, movement, settlement, and military expeditions contributed to the triumph of the capitalist order. They created a new demand for the equipment of peace and war; and by wresting people from their ties to home and community and exposing them to new sights, ideas, and opportunities, they promoted the recruitment of the commercial and industrial classes. They also changed European tastes and created new wants: the Crusades in particular renewed the old link to the exotic lands of the East—which had, in fact, never dissolved completely—and gave the trade in spices a role in European commercial prosperity that it was not to lose for centuries.

The commercial expansion that began around the turn of the millennium continued with little interruption until the beginning of the fourteenth century, when there was a kind of general pause. The output of manufactures in key centers like Florence and the Low Countries leveled off or declined, and the long rise in population slowed to a stop. The significance of these signs of fatigue is still being assessed; but there is no mistaking the impact of what followed. In 1348–1349 Europe experienced the worst pandemic in its history, the so-called Black Death, and lost a quarter to a third of its people. Mortality in the cities was as high as 65 per cent. The consequences were a temporary disorganization of all forms of social and political intercourse, the disruption of commerce and industry, a severe shortage of labor, the abandonment of land hard won from nature—in short, a widespread economic depression.

The severity and duration of this depression are also a subject of lively historical debate; as is the extent to which other factors, notably a possible contraction in the supply of precious metal, were responsible for it.[5] Be that as it may, the century and a half after the Black Death stands clearly apart from the euphoric expansion that preceded and followed. From the early sixteenth century on, European trade began a new career of growth, and this "second wind," punctuated though

[5] For a cogent statement of the depression thesis, see M. M. Postan and Robert Lopez in the *Cambridge Economic History,* Vol. II (Cambridge, 1952), 191ff. and 338ff. For further discussion, enlivened by a history of the debate, see R. S. Lopez and H. A. Miskimin, "The Economic Depression of the Renaissance," *Economic History Review,* 2nd ser., **XIV** (1961–1962), pp. 408–426; and Carlo M. Cipolla, R. S. Lopez, and H. A. Miskimin, "Economic Depression of the Renaissance?" *ibid.,* **XVI** (1963–1964), pp. 519–529. Professor Cipolla denies the existence of a depression altogether.

it has been by cyclical contractions and some longer declines, has in effect continued to the present day.

What set it off? More even than the first surge, this one was linked to territorial expansion—this time across the ocean, in the New World and the Orient. The Americas contributed primarily bullion, in unheard-of quantities, swelling the money supply and making possible an even greater expansion of commercial credit. The Orient contributed its old staples—spices, silks, cottons—but in greater quantities and on a more direct, hence more profitable, basis. The sixteenth century saw the beginnings of world, as against international, trade.

In this enlarged arena, new commercial powers came to the fore. The first fruits of maritime expansion—the spices of the Indies, the silver of the Americas—went to the Iberian countries. But for complex and still-debated reasons, these were not able to convert their newfound wealth into lasting economic growth. They spent it rather on the ambitions of empire, on the food they could not grow, on the manufactures they could not make for themselves. The great beneficiaries of this surge of demand were the producers of northern Europe and the middlemen of the Low Countries. Antwerp in the sixteenth and Amsterdam in the seventeenth century served as commercial turntables, where grain, metals, fish, timber, naval stores, textiles, and hardware met the bullion of the New World. The "riches of the Indies" ran through the fingers of Spain and Portugal to swell the coffers and nourish the economies of northwestern Europe.

For all this growth of output and trade, the supply of money grew even faster, and prices multiplied over the course of a century by about three times.[6] This increase seems mild by comparison with the runaway inflations made possible by paper money and the printing press. But it had drastic consequences for European society of the sixteenth century. It hit hardest those sections of the population whose incomes were fixed by contract or custom (thus, landowners who had let their

---

[6] The attribution of this inflation to the influx of bullion from the New World goes back to Jean Bodin, social and political philosopher of the sixteenth century. The modern scholarly demonstration of the link was offered by Earl J. Hamilton, *American Treasure and the Price Revolution in Spain, 1501–1650* (Cambridge, Mass., 1934).

Since Hamilton's work, this monetary interpretation of the inflation has been almost universally accepted. It has, however, been attacked, particularly in recent years, by those who would emphasize the effect of population growth on demand. See Jerome Blum, "Prices in Russia in the Sixteenth Century," *Journal of Economic History*, **XVI** (1956), pp. 182–199; and Ingrid Hammarström, "The 'Price Revolution' of the Sixteenth Century: Some Swedish Evidence," *Scandinavian Economic History Review*, **V** (1957), pp. 118–154.

land on long-term or even lifetime leases); and those workers who were
unable to secure wage increases in proportion to the rise in the cost
of living. It has been argued, notably by Earl J. Hamilton, that this
gap between wages and prices was a principal factor in the promotion
of capitalism, by permitting a higher rate of profit and a more rapid
accumulation of capital.[7] The argument received a particular impetus
because it was taken up by John Maynard Keynes. The Hamilton thesis
has come under sharp attack, however, and the substance of one
critique, by the Marxist historian Pierre Vilar, is reprinted in this
volume.[8]

The shift of the center of commercial gravity from South to North
has also been attributed, in greater or lesser degree, to spiritual causes.
Perhaps no historical thesis has aroused more debate than that which
links the commercial success of northern Europe to the rise of Protestantism and, with it, of an ethic favorable to assiduity and tenacity in
business. And no thesis has been pronounced dead so often.[9] Yet the
alleged cadaver refuses to lie still for burial. The so-called "Weber
thesis" and its variants continue to exercise the minds of first-rate
scholars and to stimulate fruitful research into the economic history of
modern Europe.

[7] E. J. Hamilton, "American Treasure and the Rise of Capitalism (1500–
1700)," *Economica*, n.s., **IX** (1929), pp. 338–357; "Profit Inflation and the
Industrial Revolution, 1751–1800," *Quarterly Journal of Economics*, **LVI** (1941–
1942), pp. 256–273.

[8] The Hamilton thesis was criticized as early as 1936 by John U. Nef, "Prices
and Industrial Capitalism in France and England, 1540–1640," *Economic History
Review*, **VII** (1936–1937), pp. 155–185. Nef argued that the fall in real wages
was not so great as had been supposed; that had it in fact been so great, the
increase in profits would soon have been interrupted by a fall in effective demand.
It was not so much the *general* price inflation that counted, Nef asserted, but
differential increases that created an incentive to technological change. For
Hamilton's reply, see his presidential address to the Economic History Association:
"Prices as a Factor in Business Growth: Prices and Progress," *Journal of Economic
History*, **XII** (1952), pp. 325–349.

A more direct and detailed assault on the Hamilton thesis has been made by
David Felix, "Profit Inflation and Industrial Growth: The Historic Record and
Contemporary Analogies," *Quarterly Journal of Economics*, **LXX** (1956), pp. 441–
463. Hamilton has replied in "The History of Prices before 1750," in XIᵉ Congrès
International des Sciences Historiques, *Rapports*, Vol. I (Uppsala, 1960), pp.
144–164.

[9] George C. Homans, commenting on Kurt Samuelsson, *Religion and Economic Action: The Protestant Ethic, the Rise of Capitalism, and the Abuses of
Scholarship* (New York, 1961), wrote (according to the book jacket): ". . . many
students of the social sciences will be interested in this book by an able economic
historian, which does not just tinker with Weber's hypothesis but leaves it in
ruins."

It is called the Weber thesis because—although an apparent link between Protestantism and economic success had been noted as far back as the seventeenth century—the first systematic and scholarly analysis of the link was offered by Max Weber in his seminal essay of 1904–1905: "Die protestantische Ethik und der Geist des Kapitalismus." [10] Very briefly, Weber's argument was that the doctrine of predestination, characteristic of the Calvinistic branches of the Protestant movement, planted in the mind of the believer a severe anxiety concerning his salvation. One might have expected the response to be a mood of fatalistic resignation. Instead, Weber says, the Calvinist was moved to seek ways to reassure himself about his fate. In particular, he sought to live the kind of life that would presumably characterize the elect—a life of order and restraint, of diligent devotion to one's calling, a life free of distraction, luxury, and pleasure. Such a way of life, of course, was conducive to rapid accumulation of capital, rational behavior, and success in business; and one can find entrepreneurs of all faiths who chose to live this way because this was the way to wealth. Weber's point, however, is that for the Calvinist, the means became an end. The way of life became an ethic, a moral value in itself. The effect was to instill these virtues more profoundly and spread them more widely among Calvinists than among other groups. Moreover, argues Weber, once the ethic acquired its own value, it no longer depended for its nourishment on the pristine faith in predestination. It had become secularized and was able to survive the subsidence of the religious enthusiasm of the first two centuries of Protest and Reform.

Weber, it should be noted, was not a monist. He never argued that Protestantism alone made capitalism; indeed he specifically adduced other factors to complete his explanation of the development of a modern industrial economy: the rise of the modern nation-state resting on a professional bureaucracy; the advances in science; the triumph of the rationalist spirit. But he came to the problem of capitalism with a worldwide perspective. He wanted to know why industrial capitalism appeared in the West, specifically in northwestern Europe, and not for example in China, which only a few hundred years before had been far richer and far more advanced politically, economically, and technologically. And he found that Protestantism was one of the salient differentiating characteristics.

Attacks on the Weber thesis have come from several directions.

[10] Translated by Talcott Parsons as *The Protestant Ethic and the Spirit of Capitalism* (London, 1930).

Some have simply argued that no empirical link exists between Protestantism and economic success.[11] This position does not accord with
the facts, however. There is no gainsaying that, within the commercial
sphere of northwestern Europe, the mantle of leadership did shift in
the second half of the sixteenth century from Catholic Antwerp to
Protestant Amsterdam; that on the whole, the industries of Britain and
Holland overshadowed in growth and technological dynamism those of
Italy and other southern producers; and that in countries of mixed
religious allegiance, like France or the Rhineland, the Protestants came
to play a role in trade and manufacturing far out of proportion to their
numbers. On the other hand, one can easily cite instances of thriving,
energetic Catholic centers—the wool towns and villages of Flanders,
for example, or the metalworking city of Liège. The data are not so
one-sided as they sometimes appear; but the weight of the evidence is
still on one side.

To note this, however, is not to prove Weber's thesis; correlation
is not equivalent to cause and effect. Some have argued that it is not
a Protestant ethic that made the fortune of Calvinist businessmen, but
their situation as a persecuted minority, cohesive even when dispersed
in space and excluded from honorific, noncommercial occupations.[12]
Others have sought an explanation in the special circumstances of
Protestant childrearing and education.[13] Still others have reversed the
relationship entirely and argued that it was not Protestantism that promoted capitalism, but rather capitalism that shaped Protestantism to
its taste and purpose.[14] The last position is particularly attractive to
Marxist historians, who view the economic system as the foundation
of the institutional order, and the rest—religion, government, arts, and
letters—as a derivative superstructure. It is all the more interesting,
therefore, to read a recent essay by a leading Marxist historian which

[11] See Samuelsson, *op. cit.*, or G. R. Elton, *Reformation Europe 1517–1559*
["The Fontana History of Europe"] (London, 1963), pp. 311–318.
[12] For an analysis of the success of Calvinists—and similar groups—in international trade and banking in terms of their minority status, see David S. Landes,
Bankers and Pashas: International Finance and Economic Imperialism in Egypt
(Cambridge, Mass., 1958), pp. 16–28. The more complex intergenerational model
of Everett Hagen, *On the Theory of Social Change: How Economic Growth
Begins* (Homewood, Ill., 1962), is essentially a variant. Hagen seeks to trace
the economic consequences of loss of status and of discrimination through their
effects on personality and motivation.
[13] This is the approach of David C. McClelland, *The Achieving Society*
(Princeton, 1961), who lays primary stress on the inculcation of so-called "need-
achievement," which is psychological jargon for the need to achieve.
[14] For example, H. M. Robertson, *Aspects of the Rise of Economic Individualism* (first published, Cambridge, 1933; reprint, New York, 1959).

treats the relationship between Protestantism and capitalism as one of reciprocal influence and reinforcement (Christopher Hill, "Protestantism and the Rise of Capitalism").[15]

At this point, we may attempt a historical definition of capitalism as it developed over these first six or seven hundred years, that is, to about the end of the seventeenth century. This was the era of so-called *commercial capitalism,* that is, a capitalism dominated by commercial activity. This is not to say that there was no capitalistic industry; on the contrary, the textile manufactures of late medieval Italy and Flanders were organized by typically capitalistic entrepreneurs, who owned the instruments of production and employed, among others, completely dependent workers, skilled and unskilled, who constituted a true proletariat. Moreover, the effect of continuing technological advance—for example, the introduction of the blast furnace in iron manufacture and the substitution of coal for wood in a variety of processes (brewing, soapmaking, glassmaking, dyeing)—was to require a heavier investment in fixed plant and promote large-scale industrial enterprise. Here England was the leader, making such rapid gains in the period 1540–1640 that John U. Nef characterized them as "an early industrial revolution." [16]

Yet such industrial enterprises were exceptional. Within the modern, capitalist sector—which was, it must be remembered, even at the end of our period only one part of the larger economy and the smaller part at that—most profit came from trade and finance rather than manufacturing. Moreover, by far the larger part of the goods in trade was obtained from the traditional sector—from agriculture, home work, or craft work. Even within capitalist industrial enterprises—that small sector within a small sector—the bulk of investment was in stocks of raw materials for working, commodities for exchange, or in cash for day-to-day expenditures—purchases, wages, and the like—rather than in plant and equipment for production.

In the meantime, the volume of trade was growing steadily. It grew at home, partly because numbers were increasing and wealth accumulating, partly because the process of specialization continued and an

---

[15] R. H. Tawney, in his classic *Religion and the Rise of Capitalism* (New York, 1926; paperback reprint, New York: Penguin, 1947) argues along similar lines. For Tawney, religion was initially not a stimulus to capitalism, but a restraint; it was the secularization of business—its withdrawal from the sphere of religious authority—that freed the energies of the entrepreneur. But once Calvinism did develop an ethic favorable to business and the businessman, this ethic served as a sanction for enterprise and an armor against the scorn or temptations of other ways of life.

[16] John U. Nef, *The Rise of the British Coal Industry* (2 vols.; London, 1932).

ever greater proportion of the population was being drawn into the commercial nexus. Nowhere were these trends so strong as in Britain, where geography, society, and politics favored the formation of a national market and the interpenetration of rural and urban economies. And it grew overseas, as the motif of imperialist dominion changed from looting and plunder to the cultivation of a continuing trading relationship. The sixteenth and early seventeenth centuries were the age of silver and gold; the late seventeenth and eighteenth were an age of sugar, tobacco, and slaves. In the warmer areas of North America, plantations based on forced labor grew cash crops for the European market; in the more temperate regions, an economy very similar to that of Europe, though poorer and more primitive, throve and expanded. Both areas provided important outlets for the wares of the mother countries. The great beneficiaries were France and, even more, Britain, whose overseas possessions grew partly by their own dynamic, partly as the result of a series of successful wars climaxed by the highly profitable Peace of Paris of 1763.

Finally, one must not overlook the trade among the European nations; for important as the colonial markets were, the largest and wealthiest body of consumers in the world—everything is relative—was to be found in the home countries. Here again, Britain made out best. Her supply of the best and cheapest wool in Europe gave her a critical advantage in the manufacture of the chief staple of international trade —an advantage reinforced by early and extensive recourse to cheap rural labor in the production of the cloth itself. The more backward countries of central and eastern Europe, as well as those of the Mediterranean, came to rely increasingly on British wares, supplying in return food, raw materials, and semimanufactures: naval stores and timber from the Baltic; grain from east-Elbian Germany and Poland; iron from Sweden and Russia; cotton, raisins, wine, and silk from the Levant.

This growing volume of trade accentuated at first the commercial aspect of still-expanding capitalism. But it carried with it the seeds of a drastic change in the character of this modern sector, for it put increasing pressure on the supply of manufactures and eventually called forth that fundamental technological breakthrough that we call the Industrial Revolution. And this revolution in turn led to the dominance of the industrial aspects of capitalism, whether in terms of share of investment, numbers employed, value added, or share of income. It is this new economy ushered in by the Industrial Revolution that is usually

designated as *industrial capitalism* and that Marx thought of as capitalism *tout court.*

In order to understand this transformation, one has to go back
and reexamine the industrial sector of the medieval economy. In the
beginning—in the eleventh and twelfth centuries—production for
market was almost entirely the work of independent craft shops, with
master often assisted by one or more journeymen or apprentices. Fairly
early, however—as far back as the thirteenth century—this independence
broke down in many areas, and the artisan found himself bound to
the merchant who supplied his raw materials and sold his finished
work. This subordination of the producer to the intermediary (or, less
often, of weak producers to strong ones) was a consequence of the
growth of the market. Where once the artisan had worked for a local
clientele, a small but fairly stable group that was bound to him per-
sonally as well as by pecuniary interest, he now came to depend on
sales through a middleman in distant, competitive markets. He was
ill-equipped to cope with the fluctuations inherent in this arrangement.
In bad times he might be completely idle, with no one to sell to; and
when business improved, he usually had to borrow from his merchant
the materials needed to get started again. Once caught on a treadmill
of debt—his finished work mortgaged in advance to his creditor—the
craftsman rarely regained his independence; his work sufficed to support
him—no more—and he was in fact if not in principle a proletarian,
selling not a commodity, but labor.

Aside from his pecuniary difficulties, the local artisan was in no
position to know and exploit the needs of distant consumers. Only the
merchant could respond to the ebb and flow of demand, calling for
changes in the nature of the final product to meet consumer tastes,
recruiting additional labor when necessary, supplying tools as well as
materials to potential artisans. It was largely in this way that the rural
population was drawn into the productive circuit. Very early, urban
merchants came to realize that the countryside was a reservoir of cheap
labor: peasants eager to eke out the meager income of the land by
working in the off-season, wives and children with free time to prepare
the man's work and assist him in his task. And though the country
weaver, nail-maker, or cutler was less skilled than the guildsman or
journeyman of the town, he was less expensive; for the marginal utility
of his free time was, initially at least, low, and his agricultural resources,
however modest, enabled him to get by on that much less additional
income. Furthermore, rural industry was free of guild restrictions on

the nature of the product, the techniques of manufacture, and the size of enterprise.[17]

The result was the putting-out system, so called because merchant-manufacturers "put out" raw materials—raw wool, yarn, metal rods, as the case might be—to dispersed cottage labor, to be worked up into finished or semifinished products. Sometimes the household was responsible for more than one step in the production process: spinning and weaving were a typical combination. But the system was also compatible with the most refined division of labor, and in the cutlery manufacture of Solingen or Thiers or in the needle trade of Iserlohn, the manufacturing process was broken down into as many as a dozen stages, with each cottage shop specializing in one.

Putting-out was a major step on the path to industrial capitalism. For one thing, it brought industrial organization closer to the modern division between employers who own the capital and workers who sell their labor. To be sure, most domestic weavers owned their loom and nailers their forge.[18] They were not, however, independent entrepreneurs selling their products in the open market; rather they were hirelings, generally tied to a particular employer, to whom they agreed to furnish a given amount of work at a price stipulated in advance.[19]

For another, putting-out made possible a substantial expansion of production without the penalty of labor bottlenecks. The cost of manufacture fell and with it the price of the finished goods. This in turn stimulated demand, and this then elicited a further expansion of output. Thus was renewed on a much larger scale the upward spiral that had marked the initial breakthrough from the medieval subsistence economy to a capitalist system of specialization and exchange.

Finally, putting-out made an important indirect contribution to the rise of industrial capitalism. The introduction of manufacture into agricultural communities drastically increased the size of population that could be supported, and destroyed forever the traditional balance

---

[17] The discussion of the industrial sector of the medieval economy is based on D. S. Landes, "Technological Change and Industrial Development in Western Europe, 1750–1914," *Cambridge Economic History,* Vol. VI (Cambridge, 1965), pp. 276–277.

[18] When the equipment was especially costly, however, the merchant was likely to own it and rent it to his employees. This pattern was common in Nottingham, for example, after the invention of the stocking frame. Since, moreover, the merchant favored with his orders those workers renting his frames, the independent contractor was hard pressed to survive.

[19] This dependence was also true of many urban workers; as noted earlier, the great Italian and Flemish textile centers of the Middle Ages were characterized by a sharp cleavage between capital and labor.

between numbers and area. Swollen villages of a thousand and more inhabitants, many of them wholly or almost wholly dependent on industry, found it impossible to maintain the old social fabric, which was tied to widespread land ownership and shared communal rights. The whole process of dissolution was hastened by the dynamic, self-reinforcing character of the intrusion. New sources of income meant earlier independence for minor children, earlier marriage, and larger families. Population grew faster, and surplus labor both attracted industry and increased dependence on it. The effect was to promote occupational specialization and hasten the absorption of the countryside into the capitalist economy. The best—almost the only—study of the larger social as well as economic consequences of putting-out is Rudolf Braun's "The Impact of Cottage Industry on an Agricultural Population," extracts from which are reprinted in this volume.

The great exponent of the putting-out system was England, where by 1500 more than half the output of wool cloth was of rural manufacture; in Flanders, this development was also early. But in the rest of Europe, the opposition of the guilds, which were sustained by governments that saw in them a source of revenue and an instrument of social control, was a tenacious barrier to change. Thus France and western Germany did not see a wide extension of cottage industry until the eighteenth century; and Italy, which was dominated by city-states, never really effected the transition.[20]

Putting-out had its limits, however, and it had reached them in England by the eighteenth century. Geographical enlargement of the area of manufacture had continued to the point of steeply rising transport costs; while the effort to squeeze more work out of the existing labor force was thwarted by the workers' high preference for leisure once a certain level of income was achieved. Moreover, the greater the demand for manufactures, the greater the incentive of the cottage worker to appropriate the raw materials furnished by the employer and work them up for his own benefit. Efforts to compel honesty and performance by fines, imprisonment, and even corporal punishment were of no avail.

The answer was finally found in a new technology—the Industrial Revolution. It consisted in a cluster of major innovations: the substitution of machines for human skill and strength; of inanimate for animate

[20] For a suggestive study of the disastrous consequences of guild conservatism for Italian industry, see Carlo M. Cipolla, "The Decline of Italy: The Case of a Fully Matured Economy," *Economic History Review*, 2nd ser., **V** (1952), pp. 178–187.

sources of power (the water wheel, but even more, the steam engine); and of new, more abundant raw materials for those traditionally used (thus, the replacement of charcoal by coke in iron smelting); and the organization of work in compact units under supervision—the factory system.

The factory deserves special attention. It is sometimes assumed that the distinguishing characteristic of the new form was the separation of the functions of capital and labor; but as we have seen, this separation was already characteristic of the putting-out system. Others have seen the essence of the factory in the use of machinery and the introduction of a central source of power, whether water wheel or steam engine. This interpretation comes closer to the facts, for the triumph of concentrated over dispersed manufacture was indeed made possible by the economic advantages of power-driven equipment. The factory had to beat cottage industry in the marketplace, and it was not an easy victory.

Yet the use of a central power source does not necessarily entail recourse to factory organization. Thus in nineteenth-century Coventry, steam engines were used to drive the machines of dozens of independent weavers, each working in his own cottage or garret.[21] Even more common was the practice of leasing space and power in a mill to individual artisans, each conducting his own enterprise. Nor does the availability of decentralized power entail the dissolution of the factory. To be sure, the invention of the electric motor has permitted small shops and dispersed craftsmen to compete with larger productive units; but these larger units have also been quick to profit from the convenience and flexibility of the new form of energy.

No, the essence of the factory is discipline—in the opportunity it affords for the direction and coordination of labor. It was in this respect that the putting-out system was weakest; indeed, nothing testifies so well to the revolutionary character of the new arrangements as the great reluctance of the workers of the late eighteenth and early nineteenth centuries to abandon their cottages or shops and enter the mills. It took several generations to form a punctual, efficient factory labor force. And nothing conveys better the economic contribution of the new arrangements than Neil McKendrick's essay on the Wedgwood factory—an example the more impressive precisely because this was as yet an unmechanized enterprise.

These technological innovations made possible unprecedented gains

[21] See John Prest, *The Industrial Revolution in Coventry* (Oxford, 1960). Prest calls these "cottage factories."

in productivity and set in motion a spiral of lower costs, increasing demand, and economic growth more powerful than any before or since. This thesis is the burden of Donald C. Coleman's "Industrial Growth and Industrial Revolutions": the uniqueness of *the* Industrial Revolution, that crucial breakthrough from a preindustrial to an industrial economy.

The process of investment and expansion was not one of balanced advance. In the beginning, the leading role was played by textiles, the most important manufacturing industry in terms of numbers employed, investment, or output, and the locus of the new mode of production. Eventually it passed the baton on to other branches: metallurgy and railroads in the middle of the nineteenth century; electrical engineering, chemicals, and automobiles at the beginning of the twentieth. But in those critical decades of transition, the critical demand pressure for technological change was felt in the light consumer industries; and to this day these constitute the most convenient entry way to industrialization.

With time, these initial technological changes spread more widely through the economy. Machines that were effective in cotton were adapted to wool, linen, and silk; chemical processes that were designed to produce alkalis required acids or threw off by-products that found their own industrial uses; the principles utilized in metal-shaping machinery found application in other branches—in cutters for leather work, stamps and presses for ceramic and rubber manufacture. Above all, power—essentially steam power—was introduced everywhere and, as the solidarity and precision of machinery increased, drove the wheels of industry ever faster. The most spectacular of these advances occurred, ironically enough, not in industry but in transport. This was the railroad, which was the product of a combination of innovations: the high-pressure steam engine, for driving; the coke-blast furnace and puddling, for cheap rails; machine tools, for accurate shaping of the parts; advances in mining, for cheap fuel; and advances in lubrication, for fast operation. The whole process was mutually stimulating and self-sustaining. Change was built into the system.

The process of change grew faster with time, as the corpus of modern techniques grew, and with it, the opportunities for the discovery, by analogy or serendipity, of new applications of old principles. Moreover, in the course of the nineteenth century, the relations between science and technology grew closer, to their mutual advantage. In the early decades of the Industrial Revolution, technique was essentially empirical; most advances were made by ingenious but scientifically innocent tinkerers. Indeed, the stimulus to inquiry went more from industry to science than the reverse. But if empiricism was feasible, up to a point, in fields like textiles and metal work, it was far less productive in chemistry and less yet in electricity. The new industries of the nineteenth century became increasingly dependent on scientific research for answers to the problems of the shop and factory; meanwhile autonomous advances in pure science generated their own harvest of practical applications.

These technological advances produced fundamental changes in the structure of society and the institutional order; and indeed, it is in this wider sense of an institutional order that Marxists and many others use the word *capitalism*. The modern industrial sector grew steadily, partly by creating new demands, partly at the expense of the older branches of manufacture. (This process was at times extremely painful; the most notorious case is the agonizing decline of the hand-loom weavers under the pressure of competition from the power loom.) With growth and the shift from older forms of dispersed manufacture to factory production came a redistribution of population. New industrial cities mushroomed—overcrowded, jerry-built, dirty, noisome. A new proletariat arose, more numerous, concentrated, and class-conscious than the old; and a new "chimney aristocracy" challenged the landed gentry for status and power.

In the economic sphere proper, the new techniques brought with them a massive shift from variable capital (working cash, stocks of raw materials, and finished goods) to fixed capital (plant and equipment).[22] Along with this went an increase in the scale of manufacture. The pioneer enterprises of the Industrial Revolution were generally small, even tiny, and grew mainly by reinvesting earnings. Later entrants were larger, and by the middle of the nineteenth century, new enterprises in capital-intensive industries like mining, iron, or engineering were too big for the purses of a single businessman or small group of partners. Instead, entrepreneurs had recourse to joint-stock arrangements, in particular, the limited-liability corporation. This trend was delayed in Britain, where the early start in the days of rudimentary, relatively cheap machinery permitted her industrial firms to begin small and grow with success. It was more marked on the Continent, especially in Germany, where rapid industrialization did not begin until about 1850 and then concentrated far more than in Britain in the capital-

---

[22] On the preponderance of variable capital in the early years of the Industrial Revolution, see Sidney Pollard, "Fixed Capital in the Industrial Revolution in Britain," *Journal of Economic History,* **XXIV** (1964), pp. 299–314.

intensive branches. The triumph of the new business form is the theme of David Landes's essay on "The Structure of Enterprise."

A late industrializer like Germany not only needed more capital; because of her economic backwardness, she had less to work with. Even using the joint-stock principle, the German business community could not have assembled unaided the resources needed to build modern industrial plants. An institution had to be created to raise these funds by tapping the savings of a broader stratum of the population. This institution was the investment bank. Invented in Belgium in the 1830's, popularized by French entrepreneurs in the 1850's, these finance companies (as the English called them) or *crédits mobiliers* found their widest acceptance and greatest field of action in Germany. There they took the form of mixed banks, on the one hand accepting commercial deposits, on the other using these short-term assets to finance long-term investments. They promoted industrial enterprises, sold their shares, held blocks of stock in their own portfolios, lent their "protégés" money as needed, and retained a direct hand in their operations by placing representatives on their boards of directors. Some of these banks came to influence or control in this way dozens of the largest firms in Germany. Not coincidentally, German writers were the first to suggest that a new business system had arisen, which they dubbed *finance capitalism*.

The German experience, of course, is only one example of a widespread problem, particularly acute today: how to overcome backwardness and catch up with earlier industrializers. It is a problem that all the countries of Europe have had to solve, each in its own way. And it is this European achievement that is the basis for Alexander Gerschenkron's reflections on "Economic Backwardness in Historical Perspective."

This growth of industrial capitalism was necessarily uneven. Investments rose and fell with market prospects and the state of credit, and with them employment and income. Instead of the irregular and largely adventitious ups and downs of the "preindustrial" economy, determined largely by the character of the harvest, a pattern of fairly regular short-run (seven- to ten-year) fluctuations developed, which has come to be known as the business or trade cycle; and alongside these, intercyclical variations in specific branches such as building, of roughly twenty years; and then longer irregular waves, whose significance is a matter of investigation and dispute.[23] Thus the most

[23] The best introduction to the nature and historical record of economic fluctuations remains Joseph Schumpeter, *Business Cycles* (2 vols.; New York, 1939).

prominent feature of these long waves is an upward or downward trend of prices; and it is still not clear whether these price movements are cause or symptom of structural changes in the economic system. In any event, depending on the theoretical model employed, the European economy of the modern period may be seen as traversing at least two and a half such long waves: inflation, 1790–1817; deflation, 1817–1848; inflation, 1848–1873; deflation, 1873–1896; inflation, 1896–1929 (or possibly 1896–present, with the sharp deflation of the 1930's only a cyclical interruption). Or, the period 1817–1896 may be seen as one long deflation consequent on gains in productivity, with the price rise of the 1850's a short aberration produced by the influx of gold from California and Australia.[24]

The years from 1873 to 1896 present a special problem. Prices fell about a third, and profits with them. Nominal wages held up fairly well, so that real wages rose—for those who were employed; employment however, was more than usually precarious, and cyclical contractions were sharper and more prolonged than before. Meanwhile output rose. The period came to be known in Britain as the Great Depression, though the question remains: Whose depression? On the Continent experience varied, though even in so buoyant an economy as the German, these were often difficult years (the 1870's in particular), and entrepreneurs were hard pressed to maintain profits.

The nature of the Great Depression has been the subject of much debate. Marxists have tended to see in it a general crisis of the capitalist order, a crisis due to the inevitable rise in the proportion of "constant" to "variable" capital and hence a decline in the rate of profit. Non-Marxists, on the other hand—as implied above—treated the contraction as simply one phase in a long history of long waves; until recently the only question was whether it was produced by monetary or "real" factors, by a failure of the supply of money to keep up with demand or by diminishing costs and overproduction. In either case there was nothing particularly momentous about this protracted downturn of prices and profits.

Then in 1952 the English economist Phelps-Brown suggested an interpretation very similar in one respect to the Marxist one.[25] He

Also useful is Wesley C. Mitchell's classic, *Business Cycles: The Problem and Its Setting* (New York, 1927).

[24] An analysis of British economic history in terms of these short cycles and long trends is provided by W. W. Rostow, *British Economy of the Nineteenth Century* (Oxford, 1948). The book devotes much of its attention to the deflationary decades 1873–1896.

[25] E. H. Phelps-Brown and S. J. Handfield-Jones, "The Climacteric of the 1890's: A Study in the Expanding Economy," *Oxford Economic Papers,* **IV** (1952), pp. 266–307.

argued that the "depression" did constitute a general crisis—what he called a "climacteric"—which he attributed to a pause in the pace of technological innovation. The gains in productivity latent in the cluster of inventions that had made the Industrial Revolution had been largely exhausted and only a new burst of novelty could stimulate investment and relaunch the expansion. This new impetus, he argued, was given about the turn of the century by what has sometimes been called the Second Industrial Revolution: the advances in chemical manufacture, the introduction of electric power, the invention of the automobile. The Great Depression was thus, in Phelps-Brown's view, a great divide —not the end, but a new beginning.[26]

Whatever the explanation of these decades, the consequences and concomitants of deflation are clear. (It is Maurice Dobb's ability to see this larger picture—the economic conjuncture and its institutional consequences—that gives value to the selection from his *Studies in the Development of Capitalism*.) Businessmen everywhere bent every effort to stabilize prices and reduce competition. On the international level, an earlier trend to free trade was reversed, and prohibitive tariffs everywhere except in Britain turned national markets into sheltered preserves. Within these markets, once competitive enterprises merged to form monopolistic giants; or combined in cartels to fix prices, output, or most effectively, both. Again, the country that moved farthest in this direction was Germany—partly because the corporate structure of enterprise and the close ties between industry and banking favored these agreements; partly because the law supported and enforced what we would call arrangements in restraint of trade; and partly because the entrepreneurial bureaucrats developed by the German business system had a strong penchant for order and organization.

Finally, these decades saw an intensification of imperialistic expansion abroad; and while much of the territorial annexation of the period offered little economic advantage, the need for markets was always alleged—and persuasively—as justification. More significant of the search for new sources and higher rates of return was the swelling export of capital from industrially advanced, wealthy Europe to the "under-

[26] Phelps-Brown has been sharply criticized by D. J. Coppock, another English economist—not so much on the substance of his argument, however, as on his timing of the climacteric. See Coppock, "The Climacteric of the 1890's: A Critical Note," *The Manchester School*, **XXV** (1956), pp. 1–31; also his "The Causes of the Great Depression," *ibid.*, **XXIX** (1961), pp. 202–232. The discussion has recently been complicated by the injection of a related issue: the extent of depression in Great Britain compared with other European countries, and the reasons for British retardation. The interested student may consult with profit the pages of the *Economic History Review* and *The Manchester School*.

developed" parts of the world—not so much to the very backward areas that were the scene of the New Imperialism, as to the overseas lands of European settlement (Canada, Australia, South Africa, Argentina) and to the semideveloped nations of southern and eastern Europe. Again it is important to note that, like territorial acquisitions, export of capital was often motivated more by political than by pecuniary aims—thus the heavy French investments in Tsarist Russia. Yet political loans also were almost invariably linked to market considerations, and it was expected that the borrower would buy a good part, if not all, of his arms, rails, and locomotives in the lending country. With this went ever more energetic efforts to secure markets abroad from outside competition—by negotiation of preferences or the establishment of spheres of influence. This informal kind of imperialism was economically far more important than the more obvious enlargement of the territorial possessions of the European powers.[27]

Alongside these trends to closure of the market and imperialist expansion went another development of major significance for the capitalist system: an increased intervention of government in the conditions and conduct of business enterprise. Such intervention had an impeccable historical genealogy: in the early modern period, most European regimes viewed the economic system as an instrument of political aggrandizement and found it desirable, even indispensable, to dictate and supervise the circumstances of production and exchange. By the late eighteenth century, however, this pragmatic utilization of economic means to political ends, a system denoted as mercantilism (in central Europe, cameralism), had lost much of its ideological force.[28] And this for a good, pragmatic reason: in those societies capable of generating an abundant flow of independent entrepreneurs, free enterprise proved far more productive than privileged monopolies or regimented crafts. Britain led the way, and it is no accident that she also produced Adam Smith, the intellectual father of the new religion of laissez-faire (Wealth of Nations, 1776). Yet the term itself is French, and France had her own advocates of freedom of enterprise, the Physiocrats, who combined their arguments for a new order with a strangely nostalgic preference for agriculture as the truly productive branch of

---

[27] See John Gallagher and R. E. Robinson, "The Imperialism of Free Trade," *Economic History Review*, 2nd ser., **VI** (1953–1954), pp. 1–15.

[28] On mercantilism, the classic study remains Eli F. Hecksher's *magnum opus: Mercantilism* (2nd ed., rev.; 2 vols.; London and New York, 1955). Perhaps the best brief introduction to the subject is Charles Wilson, *Mercantilism* (Pamphlet No. 37, prepared for the [British] Historical Association; London, 1958).

economic activity. The new ideology found less of an echo east of the Rhine, largely because the backwardness of central and east European economies seemed to make government intervention and encouragement indispensable.

Even in Britain, however, where minimum government became a kind of sacred dogma, laissez-faire was never absolute. Social conscience, reinforced by the spite of conservative landowners against the rising millocracy, effected the passage of a series of "factory acts" governing the conditions and hours of work—first for parish apprentices (that is, public charges), then for women and children (that is, people unable to protect themselves), and finally, for adult males. By the same token, considerations of health and order, to say nothing of humanity, promoted municipal improvement throughout the country: better streets and lighting, proper sewage disposal, and systems for the delivery of gas and fresh water to individual homes. Even the departing emigrant was not neglected: the revelation of the abuses that flourished in ports such as Liverpool aroused a cry of protest that could not be ignored, and compelled official intervention in the shipping trade.[29]

On the Continent, the role of the state was far more important. To be sure, certain areas of control were abandoned: thus within a generation after the French Revolution, the major nations of western and central Europe had abolished, at least in principle, limitations on entry into and conduct of crafts and trades; and even in those places where this freedom of occupation remained to be achieved, an increasing portion of the economy was in fact accessible to all. Along the same line, in the 1850's the Prussian government abandoned its supervision of mining technique and output; and in the following decade, both France and the German states abandoned requirements of prior official authorization for the creation of limited-liability corporations. One could cite other examples, which together announce and sanction the coming-of-age of industrial capitalism in Europe.

Yet these Continental countries had not abandoned their traditional concern for economic stability—the unemployed were potential revolutionaries; or for economic growth—Britain's success served if anything as a goad to more active intervention. So one finds them coming to the support of private enterprise in time of business crisis; helping to finance those projects—the railways in particular—whose cost was

[29] As in the case of the factory acts, much of the impetus to reform—in this instance, the initial impetus—came from vested interests opposed to emigration on selfish grounds. See Oliver MacDonagh, *A Pattern of Government Growth 1800–1860: The Passenger Acts and Their Enforcement* (London, 1961).

beyond the means even of associations of capitalists; building divers public utilities and operating them themselves; conscripting capitalists for the role of industrial entrepreneurs; and assisting those industries and innovations that were of special interest economically or militarily.

By the last third of the nineteenth century, the balance was shifting everywhere back to mercantilism and away from laissez-faire. Everywhere the social problem was a determining consideration. The rise of a concentrated urban proletariat, living in conditions of poverty and squalor and increasingly conscious of the contrast between its deprivation and potential power, compelled state action. It was concern for the newly enfranchised working classes that finally converted the British to the idea of free, compulsory, elementary schooling in the 1870's and 1880's. And it was Bismarck's desire to pull the teeth of militant radicalism that led him to institute in conservative, Junker-dominated Germany the most advanced program of social insurance yet known. The diffusion, moreover, of parliamentary institutions inevitably encouraged party politics, with its attendant sensitivity to and concern for local interests. Hence the governments of Europe accepted an obligation to build efficient transport facilities even in those rural areas where the density of population and level of economic activity did not promise adequate returns; hence also these governments were ready to intervene in setting railway rates to ensure equitable treatment to big and little users, to the inhabitants of one district as well as another; and hence, eventually, they undertook to nationalize the railways and operate them themselves.

In short, although the decades preceding World War I saw the trend to bigness and cartelization that the Marxists have characterized as monopoly capitalism, they also saw the beginnings or renewal of the state intervention that has grown since and given rise to what some have called *mixed capitalism*. And these divergent yet concomitant tendencies go far to explain the different assessments by Marxists and non-Marxists of the state and fate of the capitalist system.

To Marxists, World War I and subsequent decades have brought conclusive proof of the accuracy of their negative prognosis. The holocaust of 1914–1918 was the first stage of that final internecine struggle predicted by Lenin in his *Imperialism: The Highest Stage of Capitalism* (1916); the fascisms of the interwar years were the anomalies spawned by a monster in its death throes; and the Great Depression of the 1930's was its death rattle.

Non-Marxists see an entirely different picture. They recognize the disastrous character of World War I, which by its destruction alone was a watershed in human history. (It also saw the birth of the first socialist country—in backward Russia, no less—and thereby posed the possibility of a collapse of capitalism, not as a result of internal contradictions, but of pressure from the outside.) And they see the depression of the 1930's as a catastrophic purgative of a system that was beginning to run out of control. The reasons for the collapse vary with the theoretical stance of the diagnostician. Neoclassicists have argued that the contraction and its severity were the result of excessive interference with the working of the free market: limitations on international trade and exchange, interference with normal price adjustments (including the price of labor), and the like. Others, particularly the Keynesians, have argued that the trouble arose and persisted in large part because there was not enough intervention of the right kind. Their position is that people were not yet able to understand that an equilibrium was possible at less than full employment, and that only a vigorous program of government spending, financed by loans rather than taxes, could have made up the gap between national product and consumption and set the economy back on a path of growth.

Both neoclassicists and Keynesians, however, would reject any inference that these difficulties were the symptoms of dissolution. On the contrary, what impresses them is that, in spite of errors of commission or omission, the economic order has shown sufficient flexibility to adjust to the conditions of an ever-changing technology and a new political era, and not only survive but grow. Their convictions on this point have been reinforced by the experience of the post-World War II decades. These years have seen the end of Empire—an event that might have been expected to bring the capitalist house down in ruins for want of the cheap labor and resources of colonial territories. And yet, without exception, the European economies have been healthier and more prosperous for the change. Indeed, the growth of some of these economies has been more rapid in these years than ever before in their history—more rapid even than that of many of their socialist competitors. This is the theme of the article by Max Ways on "The Postwar Advance of the Five Hundred Million."

To be sure, there is no reason to assume that these spectacular rates of growth can be maintained indefinitely. They depend to a great extent on a long pent-up demand for those consumers' goods, particularly hard goods, that were not bought in the depression years of the 1930's and the war years of the 1940's. Eventually, these wants will be assuaged; and the industries that satisfied them will have attained a capacity such that new growth will proceed at a much lower rate. This, indeed, is the typical pattern of industrial growth: a kind of S-curve of tentative childhood, vigorous youth, and quiet old age.[30] On the other hand, there is also no reason to believe that these "leading sectors" will not be relayed by others—old industries transformed by new techniques, or new industries unimagined today.

In the meantime, the danger of another Great Depression has been much diminished by increased knowledge of the economic system— here the key innovation has been the so-called "Keynesian revolution" —and by a general political commitment to something approaching full employment.[31] More than that, most governments are now prepared to be judged on their success in promoting economic growth (generally measured in terms of real income per capita); stability and employment alone are not enough.[32] To be sure, intention is not achievement and unemployment has not always proved amenable to economic management. For one thing, the very process of growth is ambivalent: the rise of some sectors or trades or techniques is usually bought at the expense of others. For another, the economic system is not perfectly efficient, and resources do not abandon less profitable for more profitable uses with the alacrity posited by theory. Labor in particular is not easy to move from place to place or job to job. Hence the persistence of so-called "depressed areas"—localities or regions whose particular products have lost favor or the ability to compete, but whose inhabitants cannot or will not leave for better opportunities elsewhere.

What is more, even in prosperous places and times, the poor are still with us. Definitions of what constitutes poverty are necessarily arbitrary and relative: for a country as rich as the United States, the poverty boundary (a family income of less than $3,000 a year) will run to ten or more times the *average* income of the poorer peoples of the world. Yet whatever the definition, it is clear that there remain a substantial number of people, to be counted in the tens of millions, who have not reaped the fruits of economic plenty and whose standard of living is below the margin of decency by comparison with that of their compatriots.

This is the present task of capitalism: to improve the distribution of the social product so as to secure to all the life of abundance and comfort that modern technology makes possible and has in fact

[30] See Simon Kuznets, "The Retardation of Industrial Growth," *Journal of Economic and Business History,* I (1928–1929), pp. 534–560.

[31] On the impact of the Keynesian revolution, see John K. Galbraith, "Came the Revolution," *The New York Times Book Review,* May 16, 1965.

[32] See Irving Kristol, "The Twentieth Century Began in 1945," *The New York Times Magazine,* May 2, 1965.

bestowed on the great majority of the population. The task is the easier for the steady advance of science and technology; for our better knowledge of the working of the economic system; and for our greater freedom from ideology and dogma. Capitalism has a flexibility today that it did not have a century ago. As a result, it is also less monolithic, less uniform. There has never been a purely capitalistic economy; but today more than ever there is a wide range of mixed systems, combining various degrees of private enterprise and state intervention.

On the other hand, the task is not lightened by the political as well as economic competition from socialist systems. For this international rivalry pushes all economies involved toward an abnormally heavy expenditure on armaments, and armaments add nothing to the standard of living. Moreover, the threat of war remains and, with it, the possible destruction of industrial civilization.

The danger is the greater, moreover, for the wide and apparently growing gap between those nations that have effected an industrial revolution—up to now all capitalist, with the exception of Soviet Russia and some of its European satellites—and the rest of the world. Many of these poorer nations of the so-called "Third World" have opted for socialism in the conviction that only the state can mobilize the society and its resources for economic development. They may well be right: as we have seen, capitalism can work only in a society that generates a substantial number of energetic, risk-taking entrepreneurs. On the other hand, the great disadvantage of such a decision is that it is usually irreversible. It is not hard for a capitalist society to transfer particular branches or enterprises to state ownership and management or to create such branches or enterprises. Indeed all capitalist economies have followed this course to some extent. But it is very difficult for a socialist economy to tolerate a truly independent and competitive private sector, if only on ideological grounds. And generally speaking, it is always better—in any sphere of activity or policy—to keep choices open and preserve room for maneuver.

Be that as it may, the rich countries seem to be getting richer, while the poor get children. This divergence foments jealousy and hatred, adds fuel to international rivalries, and increases substantially the danger of war. Thus, capitalism has a second task: to help the poorer nations attain a standard of living commensurate with that of the more advanced nations. Whether it can accomplish this goal remains to be seen. For the richer countries can only help. In the last analysis each society must make its own economic salvation.

DAVID S. LANDES, *Harvard University*

PROBLEMS OF THE FORMATION OF CAPITALISM *

Pierre Vilar †

Do we know more about the origins of capitalism to-day than we did thirty years ago? Statistical information has accumulated, but our understanding has not always advanced. The crisis of economic thought, not unconnected with the general difficulties of capitalism since 1929, has led some historians into theoretical over-simplifications which are necessarily unhistorical. Their models are not based on reality. . . .

I
Keynesian Theory Among the Historians: 1929–1950

(a) THE STARTING POINT: EARL J. HAMILTON.

I propose to discuss the influence of the ideas of E. J. Hamilton, though not to attack his work as a scholar, which is above criticism. In 1926 Hamilton undertook to reformulate the old question which had haunted historians and economists since the sixtenth century: what was the precise nature of the link between three obviously connected series of facts: the flooding of Europe by American bullion, the general price-rise of the sixteenth century, and finally the contem-

* World Copyright: the Past and Present Society.
This article is reprinted by permission of the Past and Present Society and with the consent of the author, from *Past and Present*, No. 10, November 1956, pp. 15–38. *Past and Present, a journal of historical studies,* is obtainable from the Business Manager, *Past and Present,* Corpus Christi College, Oxford, England.
† Pierre Vilar is Professor of Economic History at the Sorbonne and Directeur d'Etudes in the Ecole Pratique des Hautes Etudes, Paris, VIᵉ Section (Sciences Economiques et Sociales). He is a specialist in Spanish economic history of the early modern period and in 1962 brought out a path-breaking three-volume study of *La Catalogne dans l'Espagne moderne: Recherches sur les fondements économiques des structures nationales.*

poraneous transformations of economic, social and sometimes political relations?

. . . .

Hamilton's merit, in 1926, was that he went to the original sources: to that inexhaustible *Archivo de Indias* in Seville, where the smallest piece of gold and silver which passed through the "arca" of the "Casa de Contratación," the organ of Spanish monopoly, was registered. There the logbooks make possible a reconstruction of the life of the sailors, and the economy of the galleons and treasure fleets. The nearby Andalusian convents and hospitals supply admirable price-series. The first results of these explorations were published in three articles in 1928–1929.[1] As we shall see, Hamilton's later work makes it necessary to begin the discussion of his views with these articles.

They contain (i) a statistical reconstruction of the bullion arrivals (gold, silver) at Seville, of Andalusian prices and wages for a long period, 1503–1660; (ii) a brief critique of customary views on the rise of capitalism (improvements in the techniques of exchange, agrarian transformation, rise of the modern State); (iii) a much more definite critique of Sombart's and Weber's explanations in terms of "capitalist spirit," preferring the analysis of objective conditions. But Hamilton found the decisive conditions neither in the rise of merchant capital, nor in that of ground rent (which he believed to have been less than that of prices in the sixteenth century). Lastly, the articles contain *Hamilton's own hypothesis: capitalist development in the sixteenth century derived essentially from the lag of wages behind prices.*

Three curves illustrated this: that of Andalusian prices and wages, based on his own researches, that of French ones (after d'Avenel), and that of English ones (after Wiebe). Hamilton concluded as follows:

In France and England the vast discrepancy between prices and wages, born of the price-revolution, deprived labourers of a large part of the incomes they had hitherto enjoyed, and diverted this wealth to the recipients of other distributive shares. . . . For a period of almost two hundred years, English and French capitalists (and, presumably, those of other economically advanced countries) must have enjoyed incomes analogous to those American profiteers reaped from a similar divergence between prices and wages from 1916 to 1919.

[1] "American Treasure and Andalusian Prices, 1503–1660: A Study in the Spanish Price Revolution," *Journal of Economic and Business History*, I (1928), 1–35; "Wages and Subsistence on Spanish Treasure Ships, 1503–1660," *Journal of Political Economy*, XXXVII (1929), 430–50; "American Treasure and the Rise of Capitalism," *Economica*, IX (1929), 338–57.

Admittedly, in Spain, capitalism did not take root. However, in Spain precisely the gap between prices and wages was closed after 1530. Hamilton's explanation of Spanish decline was the traditional one: medieval outlook, religious expulsions, even "Iberian idleness." Nevertheless, the decisive factor in his view was the narrowing gap between prices and wages.

. . . .

(b) Critique of Hamilton's Original Presentation.

From 1932 Simiand raised queries about the relation between the influx of bullion and the price-rise.[2] Was it legitimate to correlate the absolute quantity of bullion arriving in Seville with price-indices on a single graph? Did not the parallelism of their movement reflect merely the choice of scale? Moreover, the quantity of metal in circulation must be presented on a *cumulative* graph.

Since then other objections have been raised. Carande has shown the importance of the gaps in the documents (1521–25), of the monumental frauds (1557). Other scholars have contested the general value of figures based purely on the "Casa de Contratación."[3] At least one factor has not been measured: the exports of bullion, which imperial debts compensated by an enormous system of internal, and often forced, credit. However, let us not be hypercritical: Hamilton's estimate still stands. But his 1929 graphs present a misleading simplification, though this is the picture which has become accepted to the point of entering textbooks, such as Heaton's, from which the general public derives a most elementary view: *prices rose in proportion to the mass of bullion entering Seville.* Bodin, Azpilcueta, Mercado, in their first stammering formulations of the quantity theory of money, never defined it as crudely as that.

We should be equally cautious about *the gap between prices and wages.* The curve of Andalusian wages is less reliable than that of prices. For England and France the graphs depend on very old figures (Thorold Rogers) or doubtful ones (nobody relies on d'Avenel in France to-day).[4] One may, of course, defend these approximations.

---

[2] *Recherches anciennes et nouvelles sur le mouvement général des prix du XVIe au XIXe siècles* (Paris, 1932), pp. 403–20, 457–78 (esp. 470–2), 492, 546.

[3] R. Carande, *Carlos V y sus banqueros* (Madrid, 1943) I, 145–56. V. M. Godinho, the excellent Portuguese scholar, has raised even wider objections to the Sevillan documentation.

[4] Wiebe, *Zur Geschichte der Preisrevolution des 16. und 17. Jh.* (Leipzig, 1895), relies on Thorold Rogers, *History of Agriculture and Prices in England* (Oxford, 1882–7) vol. III–VI. D'Avenel, *Histoire économique de la propriété, des*

Hamilton himself pointed out that his own immense effort at reconstructing prices only confirmed the facts already observed by Tooke and d'Avenel.[5] This is, however, not an argument against hard statistical work, which can alone penetrate the detail of regional, chronological, and concrete historical differences. But if we are to confine ourselves to broad general statements, Hamilton's 1929 thesis was hardly a revelation. As early as 1847, Marx wrote: [6]

In the sixteenth century the amount of gold and silver in circulation in Europe increased as a result of the discovery of American mines, richer and easier to exploit. The result was that the value of gold and silver diminished in relation to that of other commodities. The workers continued to be paid the same money-wage for their labour-power. Their *money-wage* remained stable, but their *wage* had fallen, for in exchange for the same amount of money they now received a smaller amount of goods. This was one of the factors which favoured the growth of capital, the rise of the bourgeoisie in the sixteenth century.

Moreover, Cantillon described the backwardness of Spain as due to the wage-rise in a masterly page,[7] which all the eighteenth-century Spanish economists knew, though they also seem to have arrived at this explanation independently. Thus an unpublished "Discurso," of 1780, says:

The conquest of America caused wages to rise from the fifteenth and sixteenth centuries, the price of foodstuffs having, at an estimate, quadrupled in the course of the century of Charles V and Philip II. Since other countries had not increased the mass of their money, their wages did not rise to any great extent, and they could develop their industry happily, while ours declined. Spain gained momentary wealth in currency, but lost her manufactures and gradually her treasure also migrated to those areas where we find those articles which are consumed, and then produced again for consumption.

Thus Hamilton's article "American Treasure and the Rise of

---

salaires, des denrées et de tous les prix en général (7 vols.; Paris, 1894): the criticism of Seignobos and Monod dismisses this work, though it may be excessively severe.

[5] "Use and Misuse of Price History," *Journal of Economic History*, IV, Suppl. (1944), 47–60.

[6] *Wage Labour and Capital* (French edn. ESI, 1931), p. 44. This lecture had originally been given in Brussels in 1847.

[7] Cantillon, *Essai sur la nature du commerce* (edn. IED), pp. 91–3. On Cantillon's influence on Spanish economists, Estapé, "Algunos comentarios a la publicacion del Ensayo . . . de Cantillon," in *Moneda y Credito* (Dec., 1951).

Capitalism" was a fine statistical illustration of a classic hypothesis, but not a new discovery. . . .

(c) KEYNES AND THE DANGER TO HISTORY.

"It would be a fascinating task," wrote Keynes, "to re-write Economic History in the light of these ideas, from its remote beginnings—to conjecture whether the civilizations of Sumeria and Egypt drew their stimulus from the gold of Arabia and the copper of Africa, which, being monetary metals, left a *trail of profit* behind them in the course of their distribution through the lands between the Mediterranean and the Persian Gulf, and, probably, further afield; in what degree the greatness of Athens depended on the silver mines of Laurium—not because the monetary metals are more truly wealth than other things, but *because of their effect on prices they supply the spur of profit;* how far the dispersal by Alexander of the bank reserves of Persia, which represented the accumulated withdrawals into the treasure of successive empires during many preceding centuries *was responsible* for the outburst of economic progress in the Mediteranean basin, of which Carthage attempted, and Rome ultimately succeeded to reap the fruit (Note: after Hannibal's conquest of the Sierra Morena), whether it was a coincidence that the decline of Rome was contemporaneous with the most prolonged and drastic deflation yet recorded; if the long stagnation of the Middle Ages may not have been *more surely and inevitably caused* by Europe's meagre *supply* of the monetary metals than by monasticism or gothic frenzy, and how much the Glorious Revolution owed to Mr. Phipps. . . . Such is a rough outline of the course of prices. But it is the teaching of this Treatise that the wealth of nations is enriched not during Income Inflations but during Profit Inflations—at times, that is to say, when prices are running away from costs." [8]

The phrases italicized show how the notion of *stimulus* insensibly turned into that of *responsible factor,* then into that of *cause;* similarly *flow* of metals became *supply* by the end of the passage. What is meant, in any case, by "the medieval stock of metals"? . . .

. . . .

Hamilton interpreted his first hasty curves thus: "Prices rise in proportion to bullion arrivals." Then Keynes said: "When bullion arrives, prices rise above costs, profits take a turn upward, civilization follows." A curious game of hide-and-seek now began. "History shows . . ." wrote Keynes, reviving Hume's (and Saravia's de la Calle) old arguments, as modernized by Hamilton (who followed Wiebe and d'Avenel). "Keynes, using Hamilton's material, has confirmed one of

[8] J. M. Keynes, *A Treatise on Money* (2 vols.; New York, 1930), II, 154.

his best-established theses". . . . "In this argument I follow Keynes". . . . "As Keynes shows. . . ." [9] So the historians now wrote. We enter the realm of illusions.

. . . .

The publication of the *General Theory* (1936) improved the fortune of Keynesian historical discussion. The prestige of the conservative-revolutionary thinker turned prophet led historians to accept views that I hardly apologize for presenting schematically, for that is how they invaded history. Here are some of them.

(1) PROFIT, NOT SAVINGS, STIMULATES ENTERPRISE AND HENCE PRODUCTION. When the rate of interest falls, while the entrepreneurial profit rises, times are good.

(2) PRICE-RISES CREATE PROFIT-EXPECTATION, by widening the distance between prices and profit on one hand, interest and wages on the other, and by devaluing the debts of the "active" entrepreneur to the "passive" lender. We ought therefore to favour the rise of prices (if need be by means of managed money).

(3) EMPLOYMENT became an urgent pre-occupation in view of contemporary mass unemployment. This led thinkers back to Marx, and demographic studies.

(4) MERCANTILISM, the doctrine of the influx of metal and creative function of luxury, was rehabilitated. Cantillon's views on the decline of Spain were rediscovered, and quoted.

Unfortunately, the last two themes, which might have inspired some fruitful rethinking, had less effect on historians than the first two. After 1940, Hamilton, strengthened by Keynes' support, returned to the schematism of 1929: [10]

The secular downswing of Valencian prices in 1659–89 was steady enough to be predictable and moderate enough to be absorbed in most commercial transactions, but the decline transferred purchasing power from energetic and dynamic debtors to lethargic and passive creditors. Through inventory depreciation and the impact of relatively inflexible costs, falling prices also

[9] Carande, *Carlos V*, I, 158; G. Parenti, *Prime ricerche sulla rivoluzione dei prezzi in Firenze* (Florence, 1939) 236, n. 14; C. Cipolla, "Entre Mahomet et Charlemagne," *Annales: Economies, Sociétés, Civilisations*, IV (1949), 8, are examples.

[10] *War and Prices in Spain, 1651–1800* (Cambridge, Mass., 1946), pp. 134–5. Hamilton is also the author of two monographs on earlier centuries: *American Treasure and the Price Revolution in Spain, 1501–1650* (Cambridge, Mass., 1934); *Money, Prices and Wages in Valencia, Aragon and Navarre, 1351–1500* (Cambridge, Mass., 1936).

depressed business profits, the chief source of capital at the disposal of the rising entrepreneurial class.

This conclusion did not confirm Keynes; it invoked him.

. . . .

. . . in an article of 1942,[11] Hamilton took up the schematic idea that the Industrial Revolution of the eighteenth century resulted exclusively from the gap between wages and prices. This time the statistics (English and Castilian) were extremely solid. On the other hand, the conclusions were cruder than ever:

The high level of profits raised large incomes, which always have supplied practically all the savings in a capitalistic society. As Professor J. M. Keynes has pointed out, savings without investment not only would have proved fruitless, but would have depressed business and thus limited savings. By keeping the normal rate of profit far above the prevailing rate of interest, the lag of wages behind prices stimulated the investment of savings as they took place.

In 1946, Hamilton similarly concluded his great work "War and Prices":

By involuntarily sacrificing real incomes *through the price-wages squeeze,* the labouring class bore the burden that implemented material progress, just as labourers and peasants in Soviet Russia, sacrificing through governmental directives have largely financed the mechanization of industry that was instrumental in the recent expulsion of the German invaders.

Postponing criticism, let us note the thesis: whatever the régime, capital investment requires a fall in real wages, which a capitalist régime achieves through price-rise.

. . . .

II

Objections to the Keynesian Interpretations

. . . .

(1) PROFIT AND PROFIT EXPECTATION. Historians, like economists, statesmen or trade union leaders, may usefully observe the movement of prices which encourages or discourages production. But "profit-expectation" is not the same thing as profit. "Economic man" does not long

[11] "Profit Inflation and the Industrial Revolution, 1751–1800," *Quarterly Journal of Economics,* LVI (Feb., 1942).

remain content with promises such as the short-lived illusion created by unstable currencies. We must therefore study total profits concretely and directly. All attempt to measure profit in terms of its variable components presupposes a theory of profit, which ought to be clearly set out.

(2) INTEREST. Can we say that "interest" and "profit" are antagonistic since both may increase as a result of the greater exploitation of labour? Who was right before the nineteenth century: the old economists who confused interest with "rent of money," and believed that its rate fell with monetary abundance, or the banker Cantillon, who believed the opposite? But can we investigate this matter satisfactorily at a time when different forms of interest are still intermingled: the usurer's loans for consumption purposes, loans to early capitalist production (often camouflaged as exchange operations), and loans to States and Princes, which may be both one and the other? Let us add that from the seventeenth century onwards, private enterprise rests on well-analysed combinations of loans at fixed interest and risk-and-profit-sharing investment. To oppose the "dynamic" debtor to the "lethargic" creditor is to fall into convenient abstraction.

(3) RENT. In societies where ninety per cent of the population lives on the land, can we pass lightly over agricultural incomes? Hamilton holds that in periods of expansion, rents rise more slowly than prices. All Labrousse's results contradict him,[12] as do my own for Spanish Catalonia (1716–1806): there, in spite of complications, it is clear that lords and their farmers accumulated wealth faster than prices rose: sometimes five-fold. In any case, how can we give a single solution to the problem of rent, when this depends on the length of leases; on the proportion of money payments as against payments in kind; on the "super-profits" of those who hold stocks in times of famine; on the progress of productivity; on the diminishing returns of newly colonized land, and lastly on the local variations in the evolution from feudal to capitalist rent which are affected by the differing reactions of the seigneurial community? Innumerable discussions show that 9-year leases favour farmers, 3-year leases favour owners at a time of price-rise. Labrousse has shown (what had hitherto been neglected), the immense importance of the periodic "crises de subsistances" in the history of class conflicts. Money-rents react towards price changes in the opposite way to rent in kind, and the struggle between landlords and tenants

---

[12] C. E. Labrousse, *Esquisse du mouvement des prix et des revenus en France au XVIIIe siècle* (2 vols.; Paris, 1933), II, 379–80. Between 1730–39 and 1780–89 rent rose by 98 per cent and the price of bread grain by 66–69 per cent.

may modify the proportions of each. In Catalonia, in 1793, a few steps from the French frontier, we read newspaper advertisements by lawyers offering to increase lord's feudal revenues by the mere manipulation of the old "capbreus" (land registers).

(4) COMMERCIAL PROFITS. Until the establishment of a "world market," European mercantile capitalism gambled on the exchanges between scarce products (precious and exotic, or, in time of crisis, mass consumption goods like grain): i.e. on contracts between places whose conditions of production are in no sense comparable, and on the monopoly of the carriers. It is impossible to judge these profits by the price-wage gap in the merchants' own countries. . . .

(5) THE PRICE-WAGES GAP. Let us suppose, after all, that the price-wages gap remains the chief factor in accumulation, even in these old societies. Does the curve of the "general price-level" and that of the *individual daily money wage* really give us adequate information about "profit," when the "general price level" is made up of monopoly prices (Indian spices), of the market price of grains (agitated by the "crises" and burdened with seigneurial and ecclesiastical rents), of the price of cloth (of which it is difficult, in an artisanal and corporative economy, to calculate the labour cost in daily money wages)?

But even if we grant that the market-price has triumphed, that feudal payments have disappeared, that wage-labour predominated (and by then we should no longer be in the "formative" stage of capitalism), the gap between the market-value of goods and the remuneration of the workman-producer for those goods is not the gap between an abstract "price-level" and an abstract "wage-level." We must keep a strict account of the time of labour, wages in kind (common in the old economy). The effective yield of labour is not the same in out-work, in workhouses, in industrial colonies. Finally, machines make possible the substitution of cheaper labour (women, children) for dearer, and were indeed largely introduced for this purpose. How much reliance can we therefore place on daily-wages series—even of "real-wages"—based on a few categories of workers?

Admittedly the *global remuneration of labour* and *global capital accumulation* are antagonistic. But the entrepreneur who increases the time and intensity of labour by substituting one kind of labour for another through the introduction (late though it usually occurs) of machines, may easily raise his profits, even if the wage in money-units keeps pace with prices, as Simiand has demonstrated. Marx himself argued that the demand for higher money-wages did not necessarily inhibit capitalist prosperity, and was indeed the best method of forcing employers to undertake technical progress.

. . . .

(6) THE MONETARY THESIS: INFLATION AND QUANTITY THEORY. Moreover, the Keynesian historians also hold a controversial monetary theory. This is, in the initial stages, suggested metaphorically: thus we heard of "flux" of metals, "spur" of profit. We slip into the idea that abundance of metals, or any monetary abundance, *causes* the general price-rise. This is to direct attention to an important, but not the most important aspect, of price-movements.

For *similar* price-movements make less sense than *divergent* ones. There are the differences of *place,* such as those between regions. There are differences of *short period,* such as the "social gap" between wheat and rye prices, to which Labrousse has drawn attention. There are differences of *long period,* which reveal the uneven progress of productivity and bring about substitutions: wheat is grown instead of wine, coal substituted for charcoal, etc. Let us recall Colin Clark's and Fourastié's point about the difference between manufactured goods, which undergo technological cheapening, and services—which do not.

"General movements" smooth out these internal and contradictory variations. Let us imagine an index for recent years which was to combine the price of bread with that of aureomycin: originally scarcity price, then a high manufacturing price, then (as productivity leaped forward) a low manufacturing price. Retrospective computations are open to such confusions.

Naturally "general movements" are real. The cost of living "goes up" to-day as in the sixteenth century, i.e. money will progressively buy less goods. Our problem is thus largely one of money. But let us not make the simple assumption that prices rise *because* money is plentiful, as so many recent historical writings assume. Concomitance does not imply a single causal order. There is at least a dilemma; more probably, the two things *interact.* And it is curious that historians favour a universal "quantity" view, at a time when economic theorists increasingly believe, as did Marx, that the mass of money in circulation varies with the volume of transactions and the movement of prices, and not the other way round.

But let us turn neither to theory, nor to authority, but to history. There is no increase in economic activity or in prices without its accompanying buzz of monetary phenomena of all sorts. But *what is the order of the events?* If we inject money into or keep it within a closed and inactive system, one of two things may happen: if the money is "strong" and internationally negotiable, it will flow out; if it is "internal" money, a pure fiduciary symbol, whose relations with "strong" currency are unstable, there will be an *exchange crisis.* Moreover, "strong" money never "streams" into a system *unless attracted by production.* The old economists, theologians, and monetary technicians of the sixteenth and seventeenth centuries (often the same people) were not much mistaken on these points.

But strong and internationally valid money in that period meant gold and silver. Did they *create* activity or *reflect* it? Keynes suggests the former, on the basis of ill-considered examples of "looted treasures" injected into a vaguely defined "world" without any opposite flows. But he does also refer to *mining.* And mines are not sunk, closed, or reopened at any moment. . . . Everybody knows that the "spur of profit" operated on mining entrepreneurs as elsewhere, and that the discoveries corresponded to an increased demand for money. But if any psychological or sociological symbol might have created "profit-expectation," why the stubborn search for a *commodity:* gold and silver-money? Unless we accept the idea of *commodity-money,* we shall certainly be unable to understand history, and probably also theory. Gold, a commodity and as such exchanging for other commodities, goes only where these are produced. Even in Spain, when production ceased, gold ceased to arrive or flowed out, a fact which Hamilton, Keynes, Simiand cause us to forget, since they write as if they assumed that gold was not *"bought" with anything.* We may indeed have unilateral flows of gold; but these lead to hoarding, in which case we can forget about them, for hoarding is the very opposite of investment. This point was also anticipated by Marx.

.   .   .   .

III
The Problems Reconsidered

.   .   .   .

Hamilton asks us to seek the causes of the introduction and development of capitalism in "profit-inflation," the causes of profit-inflation in price-rises, and the causes of these in the accelerated production of precious metals. Nobody denies that periods of rapid monetary devaluation, whether in 1851–57, in the sixteenth or the eighteenth centuries, represented conjunctures favourable to capital and dangerous to real wages. But the historian's business is not only to discover favourable conjunctures, but to explain the appearance of economic "structures." The appearance of capitalism required a far more complex mechanism than the simple influence of American bullion on European prices. History does not start with Christopher Columbus.

(3) CONDITIONS OF PRODUCTION AND GENERAL PRICE MOVEMENTS. The Hamiltonian model rests on the observation of the "general movement of prices." But if all prices rise, it is logical to seek the cause of this in the cost (the conditions of production) of the precious metals which serve to measure them, while remembering that the conditions of production of other commodities also change over time, and vary from one place to another. It may be useful to establish some elements of periodization for these changes.

(a) 1450–1525: before the discoveries. In Europe this was a period of major changes: of renewed population rise, after the great plagues and wars; of technical inventions (50 important ones, it has been calculated, against 43 in the eighteenth century),[13] of social crisis, such as the struggle of peasants against lords, which prepared the subsequent contrast between Eastern and Western Europe, between Castile and Catalonia. In this period the current European products were cheap, metals and exotic products at a premium. Hence the passion for discovery and overseas trade. If Castile came to the fore then, it was because it was, from the fifteenth century on, a dynamic and creative country, with its association of sheep-breeders (the Mesta), its Andalusian and Basque navy, its fairs (e.g. at Medina). Thus the fact that the new metals arrived through Spain is consequence as much as cause.

(b) 1525–1600: the price-rise. We distinguish three elements in the conditions of production of American metals: (i) looting, (ii) forced labour and (iii) technical progress (the mercury amalgam process). This drastic fall in the cost of monetary metals corresponds well enough to their general devaluation.

However, if this inflationist invasion stimulated the production of certain countries, it finally destroyed that of Spain. Hamilton says that this was because the movement of wages kept pace with prices there. But why? Once again we must thus ask questions about population, emigration, hoarding, imperial indebtedness, investments in public securities such as the juros and censos which built a pyramid of

[13] Executive Sec'y of the US Temporary National Econ. Committee, Final Report, p. 105.

parasitism,[14] monopolies such as the Mesta and the port of Seville, the internal resistance of the feudalists, the existence in Spain itself of a quasi-colonial labour force (the Moriscoes). The problems, it is clear, are complex: economic structure counts for at least as much as conjuncture.

It is equally important to compare the conditions of production in Spain with those in other countries. For the metals which enriched Spain parasitically (and therefore in the end ruined her) flowed out into those countries *where its purchasing-power was greatest*. The market was thus unified, money redistributed. But the relations between the cost of production of the metals and that of other commodities were expressed *in terms of exchange-rates,* as the Spanish theologians who meditated on interest and usury understood, if they did not explain.

(c) *Seventeenth-century stagnation.* As the sixteenth gave way to the seventeenth century, the vertical drop in colonial population which has recently been demonstrated produced its consequences: mining profits fell, mines were abandoned for agriculture.[15] This rise in the costs of silver production led to a fall in prices, in Spain from about 1600, elsewhere somewhat later. Spain attempted to meet this with a catastrophic inflation of *vellon* (mixed copper and silver, later copper) currency. Other countries reacted differently, though in general with some difficulty.

(d) *The eighteenth century.* Though its phases remain to be investigated in detail it is certain that the eighteenth century, with its price-rise and its favourable conditions for profits and capital, was also the century of revival for the Hispano-Portuguese colonial systems. Colonial mining once again profited from a numerous and available labour force. But Hamilton's model would lead us to confuse England, France and Spain, whose fortunes are not comparable in this period. If we wish to understand events in this century it is better to follow the structural analysis which Labrousse has made for France, demonstrating a dialectical process: bourgeois enrichment—popular impoverishment—revolution.

(4) THE "PRIMARY ACCUMULATION" OF CAPITAL. If capitalism is to function, moreover, capital must first have been accumulated before the establishment of a capitalist society properly speaking: private

---

[14] P. Vilar, "Le temps du 'Quichotte'," *Europe,* **XXXIV** (Jan., 1956).

[15] W. Borah, *New Spain's Century of Depression* (Berkeley, 1951) and bibliography. His figures for Mexico: 1519, 11 million inhabitants; 1540, 4–6 million; 1597, 2½ million; 1607, 2 million; 1650, 1½ million; 1700, 2 million. F. Chevalier, *La formation des grands domaines au Mexique* (Paris, 1952), 216–43.

property in the means of production and the free market must have been established, the labour-force proletarianized. How could this have taken place?

The problem is thorny. If it is difficult to imagine a feudal society evolving "under its own steam" without the help of an exogenous urban or commercial factor, it is equally difficult to believe that in societies, ninety per cent of whose members were peasants, such transformations could have taken place as it were on the margin of agrarian society.[16]

Research might therefore seek to elucidate certain key questions; the agrarian revolutions of the fifteenth and sixteenth centuries; the relative importance of feudal payments in money and in kind; the part played by the "super-profits" which agrarian sellers made during the periodically recurring famines; the problem of population and the vicissitudes of the landless labourer; and the appearance of agrarian undertakings requiring capital investment, such as irrigation arrangements, plantations, equipment for production for the market, all of which appear earlier than is often supposed. A question of particular relevance is how feudal revenues were divided, by means of the system of "adjudications" and in other ways, between an idle aristocracy and an intermediate class of "merchant-cultivators" or similar types who transformed seignorial revenues and held them ready for new types of investment; in other words how feudal revenues came to be mobilized for capitalist investment. My own work on Catalonia in the eighteenth century brings out the importance of these factors.

But if agriculture is perhaps the most obvious source of what Marx called "primary accumulation," there are others without which, he believed, the pace of capitalist expansion would have been slowed down considerably.

There is *loot* such as Spain drew from the Conquest of Granada, the African expeditions and her colonial conquests, and others from smuggling and piracy against the Spanish colonial monopoly. There is the *large-scale trade* which relied, as we have seen, on remote or temporary disequilibria of prices and not on the gap between realized values and wages. To regard mercantile enterprise in this period as a form of modern capitalism, would be as mistaken as to overlook the part which "venturing" commercial capital played in the early stages of the first great productive investments. There is *the exploitation of colonial areas* by means of slavery, forced labour or quasi-feudal

[16] For all this, Marx, *Capital*, I, ch. iii; and *The Transition from Feudalism to Capitalism: A Symposium* by Paul M. Sweezy, Maurice Dobb, *et al.* (New York: *Science & Society*, n.d. [1954]).

methods, which combined with profit by trade and profit by looting to extract wealth from the world outside Western and Central Europe for the benefit of the economically and politically advanced parts of our continent.

Such things are not merely more important than price-movements; they may provide clues to them. Thus the so-called "long waves" of prices and economic activities—the price-rise of the sixteenth, the deflation of the seventeenth centuries, etc., have long puzzled the student; some writers, like Marjolin, go so far as to regard them as "irrational phenomena." [17] But might we not see them in terms of a historic alternation between an increase in the exploitation of colonial and European labour, recalling Marx's profoundly suggestive phrase: "The veiled slavery of the wage-workers in Europe needed for its pedestal slavery pure and simple in the New World."

It is not the business of this article to suggest positive solutions to the numerous problems I hope to have raised. Its purpose has been negative: to investigate the claims of one influential method of analysing the rise of capitalism, and to demonstrate its failure to solve the problems it claimed to solve.

I would contend that the time is now ripe for erecting some sort of building from the enormous mass of facts accumulated by the German historical school, the enormous mass of figures accumulated in the past 25 years. This requires a theory of economic development; and though economists of all schools are to-day busily engaged in the attempt to construct such a theory, Marx, who first consciously faced our problem in its modern form, still provides the best guide to its solution.

[17] Woytinsky, "Das Rätsel der langen Wellen," *Schmollers Jahrbuch,* LXV² (1931), 1–42. Marjolin, "Rationalité et irrationalité des mouvements économiques de longue durée," *Année sociologique,* Série D (1938), p. 17.

PROTESTANTISM AND THE RISE OF CAPITALISM *

Christopher Hill †

I

It is over 30 years since historical thinking in this country was stimulated by the publication of Professor Tawney's *Religion and the Rise of Capitalism*. Most historians would now accept the existence of some connection between protestantism and the rise of capitalism, though Professor Trevor-Roper is a conspicuous exception. But there is little agreement on the nature of the connection. Seventeenth-century protestants themselves emphasized the fact that godly artisans had been the backbone of the Reformation, and that protestantism in its turn had proved to be good for trade and industry; and they were right on both points. Nevertheless there are still untidinesses at the edge of the thesis. The object of this article is to try to clear away some of them, by developing hints given by Professor Tawney himself.[1]

One criticism, levelled especially against Weber, is that he made inadequate chronological distinctions, illustrating the causal influence of protestantism in moulding "the capitalist spirit" by quotations from 17th century writers; even Professor Tawney relies largely on Baxter and Bunyan in his discussions of English Puritanism. Another criticism is that some of the countries in which Calvinism developed in its classical form (Scotland, Hungary) were economically backward; many aristocratic supporters of, for instance, the French Huguenots, were not at all bourgeois in origin or outlook. A third criticism is that Weber

* Reprinted in abridged form from F. J. Fisher (ed.), *Essays in the Economic and Social History of Tudor and Stuart England in Honour of R. H. Tawney* (Cambridge, 1961), pp. 15–39. Used by permission of the author and the Economic History Society.

† Christopher Hill is Master of Balliol College, Oxford. He is the author of numerous books and articles in English history of the seventeenth century. Among the more recent are *Puritanism and Revolution, Oliver Cromwell, 1658–1958, Economic Problems of the Church, from Archbishop Whitgift to the Long Parliament, The Century of Revolution, 1603–1714,* and *Society and Puritanism in Pre-Revolutionary England.*

[1] R. H. Tawney, *Religion and the Rise of Capitalism* (Penguin ed.), pp. 101–03.

and Tawney emphasised points of doctrine which would not have seemed central either to the reformers or to their critics. Protestant teachings on usury, callings, treatment of the poor, and so forth, were peripheral: granting that individual protestants contributed to the rise of a capitalist ethic by what they said on these subjects, it still has not been shown that protestantism as such is associated, either as cause or effect or both, with the rise of capitalism. If connections are to be established, they must be sought in the central doctrines of the reformers, those which most sharply differentiated them from their Roman Catholic contemporaries. And then we have to face a fourth objection in the fact that the reformers thought they found their doctrines in the New Testament and St. Augustine. Are we to regard these writings as emanations of the capitalist spirit? If not, why not? [2]

II

The central doctrine of protestantism is justification by faith. The central target of the reformers' attack was justification by works. We must begin here.

When protestants criticised the doctrine of justification by works, they were not saying that charitable works should not be performed. They were attacking the purely formal routine actions by which many Roman Catholic theologians taught that merit could be acquired— telling of beads, saying of paternosters, giving of candles. Luther distinguished between 'two kinds of works: those done for others, which are the right kind; . . . and those done for ourselves, which are of smaller value'. . . .

. . . .

Where 'good works' in the wider sense were concerned—acts of mercy or charity—a protestant thought that *what* a man did was less important than the spirit in which he did it. Justification by works led to a formal righteousness: by performing a round of good works, one bought oneself off from the consequences of sin. Grace came through the sacraments, through the miracle of the mass. Penance was imposed by the priest: it could be performed without true inner

[2] By 'the capitalist spirit' I mean something more specific than a love of money, which can be found in earlier ages. I mean an ethos which, within the framework of a market economy, emphasizes productive industry, frugality and accumulation, as good in themselves. On this definition, banks and usury are not central to the problem, since they existed before the rise of capitalism. (See R. H. Hilton, 'Capitalism—What's in a name?', *Past and Present*, No. 1).

penitence. But protestants thought the effectiveness of the sacraments depended on the moral state of the recipient. . . .

. . . A good man made a good work, not a good work a good man. Faith was 'nothing else but the truth of the heart.'

This insistence that each believer should look inward to his own heart contributed to give protestantism its fundamentally individualist bias. Papal doctrine since the 14th century had postulated a common store of grace, accumulated in the first instance by Christ, and added to by the merits of saints, martyrs and all who performed more good works than were necessary for their own salvation. . . . 'This treasure', said the Bull Unigenitus in 1343, 'is . . . entrusted to be healthfully dispersed through blessed Peter, bearer of heaven's keys, and his successors as vicars on earth . . . to them that are truly penitent and have confessed.' Individuals could draw on this treasury of grace only through the mediacy of priests, whose authority came through the hierarchy from the Pope. . . .

Justification by works, then, did not mean that an individual could save himself: it meant that he could be saved through the Church. Hence the power of the clergy. Compulsory confession, imposition of penance on the whole population—the majority of whom were illiterate —together with the possibility of withholding absolution, gave priests a terrifying power. Obedience to the Church was an obligatory part of the virtue of humility. 'If she [the Church] shall have defined anything to be black which to our eyes appears to be white', said St. Ignatius, 'we ought in like manner to pronounce it to be black.' Protestants would inculcate such blind faith in no earthly institution or man, but only in God; and fortunately God's pronouncements were more subject to argument than those of the Church. Even the Bible was checked by what the Spirit of God wrote in the believer's heart.

Justification by works meant that salvation out of communion with the Church was unthinkable. For the reformers, the direct relationship of the soul to God was what mattered: the priest, the Church as an institution, were quite secondary. So from the very beginning the protestant revolt against the Roman Church was from the nature of its theology an individualist revolt. That of course was not how Luther and his contemporaries saw it. They began by criticising specific abuses —sale of indulgences, commutation of penance. But even when they went on to attack confession and monasticism, their starting-point remained the same: a rejection of outward ceremonial enacted without a change of heart. . . .

. . . For Christians no action can be casual or perfunctory: the most trivial detail of our daily life should be performed to the glory of God, should be irradiated with a conscious co-operation with God's purposes. This was not originally to sanctify the life of all laymen: on the contrary, Luther held that the world belonged to the devil. But the true Christian could live in the devil's world without being of it, because of his saving faith.

But my motives, my intentions, the spirit in which I perform an action, are within my control. Philosophically, protestant theologians believed that the inclination of one's will towards God came from outside, from God; practically, as moralists, they emphasized the careful scrutiny of motives, the conscious attempt to see that one's will was tuned in to the divine harmonies. 'Impenitence is the unpardonable sin', declared Luther, for whom faith was 'the most difficult of all works'. Faith without a desire of repentance is as worthless as repentance without faith, wrote Calvin. No priest can search the secrets of my heart. 'Is there any angel', asked the Homily Concerning Prayer, 'any virgin, any patriarch or prophet among the dead, that can understand or know the reason of the heart?' The question expected the answer No. I, and I alone, can know whether the illuminating contact with God has been established. If it has not, all the priests and all the ceremonies in the world will not establish it. Compulsory confession cuts across the individual's direct relation to God; it is 'both tyrannical [to the sinner] and insulting to God, who, in binding consciences to his Word, would have them free from human rule.' For the godly, morality should be self-imposed: unquestioning obedience to the priest was a positive hindrance.

.   .   .   .

Luther had started more than he knew when he laid it down that the heart decides for itself. 'A man can form his own rule and judge for himself about mortifying his body.' 'Neither pope, nor bishop, nor any one else, has the right to impose so much as a single syllable of obligation upon a Christian man without his own consent, . . . for we are free from all things.' This Christian freedom makes us 'kings and priests with power over all things.' The important thing is not that Luther made such remarks, though that mattered; but that they flowed from the logic of his theological position. 'To have faith', added Calvin, 'is . . . to possess some certainty and complete security of mind, to have whereon to rest and fix your foot.' That is what protestantism gave to the 16th century man of scruple, tormented by a sense of his own sinfulness: an inner calm and self-confidence, intermittent perhaps, but firmly based on moments of elation which, once experienced, marked a man off in his own eyes from his fellows. (Hence the importance of the doctrine that the elect could never wholly fall from grace.) The tension between hyperconsciousness of natural sinfulness and the permanent possibility of God's grace expressed itself in exuberant efforts to do good works, which had nothing in common with formal righteousness. 'We teach', Thomas Taylor declared, 'that only Doers shall be saved, and by their doing though not for their doing. The profession of religion is no such gentlemanlike life or trade, whose rents come in by their stewards, whether they sleep or wake, work or play.' The godly look often into their account books and cast up their reckonings. 'But a bankrupt has no heart to this business.' For 'the Papal doctrine of doubting of God's love cuts the sinews of endeavour.'

III

. . . .

Protestantism then was infinitely more flexible than catholicism. Catholicism had the iron framework of the hierarchy, headed by the pope. It had the machinery of confession, penance and absolution, and of church courts and excommunication, not to mention the Inquisition, with which to enforce traditional standards of orthodoxy. Protestantism lacked many of these barriers to change of moral attitudes. Some of the institutions and codes of the past were retained in the Lutheran countries and in the Anglican church. Efforts were made to erect new disciplinary institutions and codes in countries where Calvinism triumphed. Desperate attempts were made to compile a protestant casuistry. But the guides to godliness, the plain man's pathways to heaven, the practices of piety, were perforce addressed to the consciences of lay heads of households. The ministers may have helped such men to discipline and educate their families and employees. But the Roman Church was able slowly to adapt its standards to the modern world through a controlled casuistry guiding a separate priestly caste, which wielded the power of confession and absolution. Protestant ministers had to tag along behind what seemed right to the consciences of the leading laymen in their congregations.

It is here, through its central theological attitude, that protestantism made its great contribution to the rise of capitalism. What mattered was not that Calvin was a trifle less strict than the canonists in his approach to usury. What mattered was that protestantism appealed, as mediaeval heresy had done, to artisans and small merchants, whom it helped to trust the dictates of their own hearts as their standard of conduct. The elect were those who felt themselves to be the elect. What was astonishing was that so many people had at the same time the same miraculous experience of conversion: thanks to God's direct intervention, grace made them free. It would indeed be inexplicable if we could not see that the psychological states leading up to conversion were the effects of a social crisis which hit many unprivileged small producers in the same sort of way. There was no salvation in the old priestly magic, because that no longer gave them any sense of control over the world of economic fluctuations in which they now had to live. Only an assertive selfconfidence could do this, and that was so novel that it must seem to come arbitrarily from outside.

> *Take me to you, imprison me, for I*
> *Except you enthrall me, never shall be free,*
> *Nor ever chaste, except you ravish me.*[3]

The social situation set large numbers of men and women seeking answers to similar problems. As, thanks to a Luther, a Calvin, a Zwingli, groups of men realised that 'the object of [Christ's] struggle was to raise up those who were lying prostrate', this in its turn redoubled their confidence. They were the elect, not only because they felt they were, but also because other people, good people, recognized that they were; and shared their views. So, once the religion of the heart spread (and the printing press, that technical triumph of the urban craftsmen, gave it a great advantage over mediaeval heresies) Lutheranism, and still more Calvinism, was a magnificent bond of unity and strength. Once touched with grace, the small group of the elect felt themselves to be unique, differentiated from the mass of mankind. Lack of numbers ceased to matter: if God was with them, who would be against them? So their numbers grew.

. . . .

IV

When the business man of 16th and 17th century Geneva, Amsterdam or London looked into his inmost heart, he found that God had planted there a deep respect for the principle of private property. The more sophisticated might express this in the 17th century by saying that respect for property was a fundamental law, or part of the law of nature (or reason): but it was easier, and more likely to overbear

[3] John Donne, *Complete Poetry and Selected Prose* (Nonesuch ed.), p. 285.

opposition, to say with Colonel Rainborough in the Putney Debates that God had commanded 'Thou shalt not steal'. Such men felt quite genuinely and strongly that their economic practices, though they might conflict with the traditional law of the old church, were not offensive to God. On the contrary: they glorified God. For here the protestant theologians had sold the pass, by their fundamental distinction between formal and charitable works, and by making the individual heart the ultimate arbiter.

The elect, Luther had said, must perform good works to help their neighbour, the community, the commonwealth, humanity; this prevents the doctrine of justification by faith giving 'licence and free liberty to everyone to do what he will.' Men serve God in their callings, however vile, because they serve their neighbour. 'A cobbler, a smith, a farmer, each has the work and office of his task, and yet they are all alike consecrated priests and bishops, and every one by means of his own work or office must benefit and serve every other, that in this way many kinds of work be done for the bodily and spiritual welfare of the community.' In his doctrine of usury Calvin always insisted that men must consider the good of the commonwealth before their own gain. It all depends on the attitude with which we go about our work. George Herbert derived directly from Luther when he wrote that labour was dignified or degrading according to the spirit in which it was done.

> A servant with this clause
> Makes drudgery divine;
> Who sweeps a room, as for thy laws,
> Makes that and the action fine.

The enthusiasm with which English Puritan preachers took up this point shows that it met a real need. It was very arguable that productive economic activity in the 16th and 17th centuries was a charitable good work in Luther's sense. The protestants' emphasis on hard work, which linked their reprobation of idle monks with their reprobation of idle beggars, sprang from the economic circumstances of the time as reflected in the thinking of bourgeois laymen. When Francis Bacon suggested that the age-old problem of poverty might at last be soluble if the resources of the community, including its labour, were rationally utilized, he was only developing an idea which he might have received from his very Puritan mother.[4] The ambiguity of the word charity

[4] See my essay on 'William Perkins and the Poor', in *Puritanism and Revolution*, p. 234; and a communication by V. G. Kiernan in *Past and Present*, No. 3, esp. pp. 49–51.

helped. The law without charity was nothing worth. Fuller said that
Edward VI's charity was no less demonstrated in his foundation of
Bridewell for the punishment of sturdy beggars than of St. Thomas's
Hospital for relief of the poor. Perkins thought the Poor Law of 1597
was 'in substance the very law of God.' Professor Jordan's remarkable
book on philanthropy in England shows how in the 16th and early 17th
centuries sober and rational calculation of what was of advantage to
the community replaced the mediaeval ideal of indiscriminate alms-
giving. The latter created beggars, and was self-regarding anyway; true
charity was to encourage self-help in the deserving.

The preachers, and still more their congregations, might well be
genuinely convinced in their hearts that industry was a good work, for
the 'common good', for 'the use and profit of mankind'; that negligence
in business harms the public state. It is a duty to God and the commonwealth to use your talents, said John Preston. Provided you do not make
gain in your godliness, provided you do not seek riches but accept them
as the blessing of God if they happen to come—then you may lawfully
take care to increase your estate. 'Ask thyself then', said Thomas
Taylor, 'what good doth my life to church, to commonwealth, to family,
to men?' It was in fact the labour of generations of God-fearing Puritans that made England the leading industrial nation in the world—
God, as His manner is, helping those who helped themselves.

Through this emphasis on the inner conviction which inspired
actions, bourgeois lay society could impose its own standards. 'God's
children look to the spiritual use of those things which the worldlings
use carnally', said Greenham. The actions of the Scribes and Pharisees
'were good in themselves, and for others', said Sibbes; 'but the end of
them was naught, and therefore both they and their works are con-
demned.' 'Man may with good conscience', Perkins thought, 'desire
and seek for goods necessary, whether for nature or for his person,
according to the former rules: but he may not desire and seek for
goods more than necessary, for if he doth, he sinneth.' ('The former
rules' include the convenient provision that 'those goods without which
a man's estate, condition and dignity . . . cannot be preserved' are
necessary.) The preachers attempted to spiritualize what men were
doing away, by telling them to do it for the right reasons. One may
suspect that their congregations paid more attention to the general
permission than to the careful qualifications with which it was hedged
around. 'They are very hot for the Gospel', said Thomas Adams of such
laymen; 'they love the Gospel: who but they? Not because they believe
it, but because they feel it: the wealth, peace, liberty that ariseth by it.'

Men are too ready to accuse Puritans of covetousness, observed William Gouge: we should be very cautious about this, since we cannot read the hearts of others, or know all the extenuating circumstances. 'Covetousness doth especially consist in the inward desire of a man, which is best known to himself. . . Observe the inward wishes of thine heart. If they be especially for the things of this world, they argue a covetous disposition.' 'When therefore thou thinkest of sparing', Dod and Clever advised, 'let not the greedy desire of gathering draw thee to it, but conscience of well using that which God hath lent thee.' 'Seek riches not for themselves but for God', was Thomas Taylor's simpler formulation. 'We teach you not to cast away the bag, but covetousness', Thomas Adams reassured his City congregation. 'O ye rich citizens', announced Joseph Hall, 'we tell you from Him, whose title is Rich in Mercy, that ye may be at once rich and holy.' When ministers went as far as that, we can imagine the simplifications and self-deceptions of laymen. The Presbyterian preachers, Hobbes noted two generations later, 'did never inveigh against the lucrative vices of men of trade or handicraft.'

The Puritans tried to spiritualize economic processes. God instituted the market and exchange, Dod and Clever assured their large public. 'He would have commerce and traffic to proceed from love', and He favours a fair bargainer. Greenham made unrepining acceptance of the market price evidence 'that thine heart is rightly affected, both to God and to the brethren.' Emphasis on the motive of the heart is the key to the preachers' distinction between 'biting' usury and legitimate commercial transactions,[5] no less than to their distinction between indiscriminate alms-giving and relief of the deserving poor, and to the protestant doctrine of the calling. All stem from the theology of justification by faith.

. . . .

V

Doctrines emphasizing the motives of the heart, allowing social pressures to influence individual conduct more freely, flourish especially, it may be suggested, in periods of rapid social change, and among those persons most exposed to its effects. Christianity arose in such a

[5] Roman Catholic casuistry, on the other hand, by its emphasis on the formal and external, made release from the sin of usury depend to some extent on methods of accountancy (H. M. Robertson, *Aspects of the Rise of Economic Individualism*, p. 164).

period; St. Augustine, on whose theology the reformers drew so heavily, also lived in an age when old standards were breaking down; and he too stressed inner motive rather than external action. 'When it is plain to him what he should do and to what he should aspire, even then, unless he feel delight and love therein, he does not perform his duty.' 'If they said that any works of mercy may obtain pardon even for the greatest and most habitual sins, they would be guilty of much absurdity: for so might the richest man for his 10d. a day have a daily quittance for all his fornications, homicides, and other sins whatsoever.' There appears to be a permanent tendency for established churches to revert to ceremonial, and for opposition groups to stress the internal element. In the Middle Ages, after the Church had become institution-alized, those who laid the strongest emphasis on the intention, the purity of heart of ordinary lay Christians, were the heretics—Massalians, Paulicians, Bogomils, Albigensians, Lollards, to whom radical protestants from Foxe to Lilburne looked back for the true Christian line of descent. This age-old protest acquired a new significance as educated townsmen, trained by their mode of life in rational calculation and independent thinking, began to challenge the clerical monopoly of education and to assert their own standards of morality. The protestant emphasis on the heart helped to dissolve the hard crust of custom, tradition and authority.[6]

To summarize the argument, then:—The appeal to inner conviction, and the rejection of the routine of ceremonies through which the priesthood imposed its authority, could have liberating effects in any society. The hold over men's minds of an established doctrinal system had to be broken before the political and social order sanctified by those doctrines could be challenged. The appeal to the heart was common to early Christianity and many mediaeval heresies. Its most obvious effects were negative. But, positively, it facilitated the evolution of more flexible doctrines. Since opposition to the Roman Church in 16th and 17th century Europe drew its main strength from the big cities, protestantism could be developed in ways which favoured the rise of capitalism. But there is nothing in protestantism which leads automatically to capitalism: its importance was rather that it under-mined obstacles which the more rigid institutions and ceremonies of

[6] The failure of full-scale capitalism to develop in 14th century Florence may be connected with lack of a thoroughgoing heresy to unite its citizens against the Church. The heretical possibilities in the early Franciscan movement were tamed by the Papacy: the big bourgeoisie who came to rule Florence needed the Papacy, for this and for economic reasons (Hilton, "Capitalism—What's in a Name?", *Past and Present,* No. 1).

catholicism imposed. The reformation mobilized masses of men against the Roman Church and the political authorities which protected it. Initial support for protestantism and especially Calvinism came from the educated minority, largely urban, which thought seriously about problems of church and state. But doctrines evolved by and for the middle class could appeal to other dissatisfied elements in the population, like the gentry of Hungary and Scotland, or the plebeians of the Dutch towns. By the same token, protestant churches were established—in Scandinavia, in central Europe—which made only slight and incidental contributions to the development of capitalism.

The protestant revolt melted down the iron ideological framework which held society in its ancient mould. Where capitalism already existed, it had henceforth freer scope. But men did not become capitalists because they were protestants, nor protestants because they were capitalists. In a society already becoming capitalist, protestantism facilitated the triumph of the new values. There was no inherent theological reason for the protestant emphasis on frugality, hard work, accumulation; but that emphasis was a natural consequence of the religion of the heart in a society where capitalist industry was developing. It was, if we like, a rationalization; but it flowed naturally from protestant theology, whose main significance, for our present purposes, is that in any given society it enabled religion to be moulded by those who dominated in that society.

'All external things [are] subject to our liberty', declared Calvin, 'provided the nature of that liberty approves itself to our minds as before God.' But Christian liberty was for the elect only. Professor Brown has argued that later Puritan attempts to spiritualize the market were the opposite of Luther's view that the world was given over to the devil. Yet the transformation was due at least as much to the victories of the protestant outlook in the world as to an abandonment of its theology. When true religion had triumphed, the godly could hardly surrender the world so cheerfully to the devil. In a society run by protestants the ungodly must be disciplined; and the duty of performing good works for one's neighbour became a duty to the community. Hence the overwhelming emphasis of later Puritanism on the religious duties of industry, thrift and accumulation. As the bourgeois virtues triumphed, so the society of largely self-employed small producers was transformed into a society of domestic- and wageworkers, who could be profitably employed only by those who owned capital. In this society the few who climbed the social ladder did so at the expense of their neighbours. So the thought of the fortunate upper ranks came to stress more and more the vices and follies of the poor. Later Calvinism in England became harsher and more hypo-critical, because of changes in society which it had helped to bring about.

. . . .

An age of ignorance is an age of ceremony, Dr. Johnson correctly observed. The victory of protestantism helped to end the animistic magical universe, and undermined the traditional popular conception of religion as propitiation. Henceforth God and the individual soul stood face to face. The sense of sin remained, became indeed more overwhelming, because sin had to be grappled with alone. But the sense of sin was now also a sense of potential freedom. No magician or priest or saint could help, but God could. His promises were free and sure. The Puritan remained terribly conscious of his own sinful nature, even whilst he tried, by careful scrutiny of motive, to identify his will with the will of God. 'It does not need modern psychology to enable us to appreciate that the more bitter the internal struggle, the more complete was the assumption of identification with the Will of God in external activities.' The simultaneous conviction of depravity and righteousness does not make the most attractive characters in the world; but it gave a vital stimulus to productive effort in countries where capitalism was developing, at a time when industry was small-scale, handicraft, unrationalized. Successful mediaeval business men died with feelings of guilt and left money to the Church to be put to unproductive uses. Successful protestant business men were no longer ashamed of their productive activities whilst alive, and at death left money to help others to imitate them. . . .

THE IMPACT OF COTTAGE INDUSTRY
ON AN AGRICULTURAL POPULATION *

Rudolf Braun †

Where natural conditions permit closed village settlements and the three-field system of cultivation, the peasant community is bound by a net of legal and customary servitudes. No man may use and till the land as he pleases. Methods and timing of work and the allocation of fields are fixed for each down to the smallest detail. It is very hard for an exogenous putting-out industry to gain foothold in so rigidly ordered an economic unit, so long as it retains its vitality. In so firmly articulated a collectivity, industry, with its individualistic character (so far as its bearers are concerned), has little play. The real three-field system with compulsory cropping stands and falls with the comprehensive and obligatory union of the villagers as an economic entity. Industrialization would destroy not only the material but also the human bases of such an economic union. As a result the village must take steps, with all the means at its disposal, to prevent an uncontrolled diffusion of industry. Its field and crop servitudes, as well as its legal and customary regulations in general, are of great service in this connection. There are strict rules about building. As long as the three-field economy is intact, so-called "out-building" is forbidden. No house may be built outside the village boundary. When possible, the construction of additional houses within the village is also strictly forbidden. These regulations give rise to endless conflicts.

Entirely different is the situation in the Highlands. In this area of dispersed farms there are no collective economic units with their rigid regulation and their ability to limit settlement and building. Rather

* Reprinted from Rudolf Braun, *Industrialisierung und Volksleben: Die Veränderungen der Lebensformen in einem ländlichen Industriegebiet vor 1800* (Erlenbach-Zürich and Stuttgart, 1960), pp. 51–69, 78–89. Translation by the Editor. Used by permission of the author and the Eugen Rentsch Verlag, Erlenbach-Zürich.

† Dr. Braun, who teaches social history at the University of Berne, is currently directing research into the problem of foreign labor in Switzerland; he has just been appointed to the University of Berlin as head of a research project on early industrialization.

the peasant has the free disposition of his land. He can use and till it as he wishes. There are no effective rules about construction or renting. In other words, whereas the village peasant must work within the collectivity and derives his security from it, the isolated farmer has much more free play. He is to a certain extent an entrepreneur, with the economic values and spirit of the entrepreneur. The specifically material characteristics of the farm enterprise—its considerable independence, its flexibility and adaptability—are in harmony with the markedly individualistic character of the farmer.

As a result, a fruitful symbiosis is possible between agriculture, with its traditional land use, and the putting-out industry of Zurich. Industrialization does not take place at the expense of agriculture. On the contrary, large areas of the Highlands are stimulated by putting-out industry in the course of the eighteenth century. Waste land is drawn into cultivation and settled; better use is made of the already cultivated terrain; the livestock improve; and so on. . . .

. . . .

Our analysis of the case of the Highlands has only limited relevance for the other areas of early industrialization in the Zurich region. . . . These other districts have their own legal, economic, and social characteristics; even geography and climate are different. Each of these districts brings to the assimilation of the putting-out system its own circumstances. Yet even so, the same factors play a role, though with different weights and patterns than in the Highlands. The same forces impede or promote the process of industrialization. All of these industrialized areas are marked by the fact that they no longer have any firmly ordered economic collectivity in the sense of the three-field system. Their legal, economic, and social structure is no longer an organic unit, with the vitality and strength to block the incursion of industry. To be sure, there remain in many places the tenurial and agricultural forms of the three-field system, with common land, the rights to the use of which are attached to the homestead and not to the person; with compulsory field use; and with prohibitions on building. But these forms no longer correspond to the reality. For one part of the population they have already become obsolete. Once the institutional order is no longer compatible with economic and social conditions, the door is open to the putting-out system. . . .

. . . .

[The significance of these considerations shows up clearly on] a map of the distribution of cottage manufacture in the Zurich cotton industry at the time of its first prime toward the end of the eighteenth century. In the year 1787 a census was made of all cotton spinners and weavers in the countryside ruled by the city of Zurich. . . . There is not—as might have been expected—a circular net around Zurich as center of distribution. Rather the most intensively industrialized areas lie in a part far off from Zurich, in the pre-Alpine zones of the Zurich domain, although these peripheral districts were drawn into the putting-out system only later and suffer from extremely unfavorable transport conditions. An examination of this map shows the strength of those legal, economic, and social forces that we have analyzed and demonstrated in this chapter as preconditions for the industrialization of the Highlands. These forces were strong enough to overcome the natural handicaps and the poor facilities for transportation. The Highlands are a back country with discrete zones of settlement, wooded glens "of forbidding aspect," inconceivably bad communications, and a rude climate. To bring the raw material in, distribute it, and ship out the finished goods was an extremely difficult task. For this reason the Highlands were only slightly touched by the first expansion of cottage weaving. The transport of the warp yarn and rolls of cloth would have been too hard. As a result, until the collapse of hand spinning, the mountainous parts of the Zurich domain remained dependent on spinning and not weaving.

. . . .

Alongside this historical treatment, however, our problem also calls for an internal analysis, since we look upon cottage industry as a mode of existence with its own explicit way of life. Such a way of looking at the problem requires us to transcend repeatedly the chronological boundaries in order to free the problem from its temporal limitations. . . .

As a point of departure for inquiry, we shall take the smallest and most natural human community, the family. The question then arises what changes industrialization made in the requirements for marriage and the founding of a family.

From the works of Gotthelf, we know that in a peasant society an engagement of marriage may have nothing of the character of an intimate, private understanding between two lovers. In a peasant marriage contract, the economic unit, with its human and material requirements, is the dominant consideration. Personal preferences have a lower priority. The main point is to maintain the organic cohesion of the enterprise. The unstable equilibrium between the work and consumption requirements of a peasant family and the size of its holdings must be assured. The result is a set of peasant marriage customs to which the individual members of the family must conform. "It thus became a custom," writes J. C. Hirzel (1792), "to leave the holdings together and pass them to the sons alone, and these in turn limited their marriages so that the farm would always be capable of supporting the family. . . . As a result we see that the population of the fertile Wehnthal has increased only little. A peasant reckons this way: my farm can feed no more than one, at most two sons; the others may have to remain unmarried or seek their fortune elsewhere."

Hirzel is describing here the so-called *Anerbenrecht*, that is, the right of testamentary preference. This practice was not confined to the Highlands particularly, but characterized the entire Zurich country-side. The tendency to give preference to one heir and to limit the fragmentation of the land was strengthened in the Zurich area in the seventeenth century by the development of communal law and rights in common. . . . In the Highlands, however, as we have seen, this feature was not prominent. Peasant marriage customs of a kind promoted by *Anerbenrecht* were most probably lacking [there] even before industrialization. . . .

The earning possibilities generated by the putting-out industry of Zurich, however, create an entirely new situation. For those men who stem from a peasant milieu (to speak of them only), there are now entirely new possibilities of marriage and the founding of a household. Industrial earnings can make a substantial contribution to a peasant enterprise. With this transformation of the basis of peasant existence, the circumstances of inheritance rights are transformed. Hirzel is clearly aware of this transformation. He writes that where manufacturing earnings slip in, the peasant alters his above-cited calculus as follows: " 'I have three to four sons; each one gets some herbage, at least enough for a cow, a bit of field, and so on. This should go a long way toward maintaining the household, and the working of this small property will leave enough time to earn the rest through manufacture.' In the end, people found that it was even enough to have a corner in the house for a spindle or a loom and enough land for a vegetable garden." The author tells us of a "worthy farmer," whom he has come to know "this year (1792)," who is cultivating only one-eighth of the holding of his grandfather and yet is living happily and well. In his *Letters on Switzerland* C. Meiners writes: "The increased and sure income offered by the combination of cottage manufacture with farming hastened and multiplied marriages and encouraged the division of holdings, while enhancing their value; it also promoted the expansion and embellishment of houses and villages. Thanks to the prospects which were opened to the farmer by his labor and that of his children, he no longer set early and anxious limits to the fecundity of his marriage. Previously fathers and sons avoided dividing fairly large and, even more, modest holdings, for they were concerned that each piece be able to nourish its holder. This fear vanished entirely with the diffusion of manufactures and cottage industry; and now the sons redivide the parcels received from their fathers, themselves the product perhaps of several divisions, because people are convinced that even a small field is enough to feed a diligent holder along with wife and children."

It is obvious that marriages are more numerous and earlier in those peasant areas where there is cottage industry. J. C. Hirzel established this fact statistically. He chose as an example the community of Fischenthal. He offers the following decennial averages of marriages concluded: 1641–1670, 42; 1671–1700, 81; 1701–1750, 113; 1750–1760, 165.

Now it must be emphasized that such marriages can no longer be called peasant marriages, for without the possibility of earning money in industry, they would never have been concluded. We must destroy the idyllic picture, which is so firmly established in the literature, of the peaceful farmer who tills his fields, milks his cows, and as a by-occupation engages with his family in a little cottage industry as well. Such a picture is not valid for the Highlands. It would convey an entirely distorted and false impression of the industrial landscape. Cottage manufacture is a by-occupation for the very smallest part of the Highland peasants (we are not speaking here of the landless cottage workers), but it is the foundation and precondition for their marriages and it makes it possible for them and their families to survive on a fractional farm holding. This comes out clearly in the synodal address of Salomon Schinz, pastor of Fischenthal: "Such a population density would never have arisen in this raw district if the substantial earnings from manufacture had not facilitated and promoted their nourishment and increase and thus doubled the number of people in half a century. If all these people are to remain here, this source of income, which in fact created them, is absolutely indispensable. Even the landowners of the middle class could not survive without these earnings, for they have piled up large debts on many parcels, either through costly purchases, or the frequent division of holdings and the consequently indispensable construction of new dwellings, or through buying out the inheritance claims of other family members—debts whose interest could not possibly be paid with the output of the soil, but only with the earnings yielded by the spinning wheel and shuttle. All of this has inevitably brought on many a disaster; when cotton earnings have diminished, the false appearance of well-being has vanished from these districts. Really comfortable landowners in my community, and also in Bäretschweil, Bauma, Sternenberg are rare; indeed, there are only a few people who can boast that only half of their lands are mortgaged. The man who has only four Gulden to pay in interest on a small parcel, big enough for a cow in summer and winter, can still make it. But any serious misfortune to his cow or his land can throw him into the class of poor, and if he has a ruthless creditor, into the class of homeless. And this latter class is frightfully numerous. Over 1360 persons in my commune must live exclusively from earnings in manufacture, and 200 households have no real property, while many have neither livestock nor chattels—their spinning wheel or loom or indispensable household articles excepted—and even the latter are lacking to the poorest."

. . . .

With these changes a whole complex of customary ways of life are necessarily once again brought into flux. Alongside the altered laws of inheritance, there develops a new attitude toward marriage. . . . A contract of marriage is no longer a treaty that determines the fate of a human and economic community down to the smallest detail. For the marriageable daughters and sons of the peasantry, these changes mean a widening of the scope of their personal pretentions. Matrimony is now enveloped in a much more intimate aura. It is a reciprocal commitment of two people, who hope with it to realize their individual happiness.

Let us now examine this development more closely in that class of the population which does not derive from a secure peasant milieu. I am referring to those economically dependent inhabitants of the Highlands whom we got to know in the first chapter, in the early stage of industrialization. It was pointed out there what the possibility of industrial earnings meant for these people. From the middle of the seventeenth century on, the demand for labor of the putting-out industry of Zurich had increased at a growing pace, and the broadest layers of the population of the Highlands had placed their fate in the hands of the putters-out, trusting blindly to the "sinister play of economic laws." In this blind confidence marriages were contracted. . . .

With pastoral indignation Salomon Schinz sketches how, in the milieu of Fischenthal cottage workers, a girl entered into matrimony: "Raised at the wheel or the loom, without knowledge of other housework or field work; daily almost in bad company until deep into the night, and when the work is over, spending the daily pay or part of it for sweets or drink, indulging every lust and not scorning for the purpose any means, however shameful, even embezzlement of the materials to be worked up or theft of wares from the house of her parents, and then entering into marriage, when compelled by necessity, often with a youngster equally light-minded and poor, owning between them neither bed nor household utensils— . . . what kind of results can be expected from such penniless marriages, where the people concerned owe the shopkeeper for the very clothes on their backs?"

We will later see that this way of life of the cottage worker, here quite negatively appreciated by Schinz, can also be evaluated in another and more positive way. The fact nevertheless remains that in these circles marriages were contracted without any thought to material considerations. "These people, who have two spinning wheels but no bed, contract early marriages fairly often," writes the pastor of Wildberg. "Beggar weddings" is the term generally used in the sources.

. . . .

Our critics with their paternal sense of responsibility, have only the material side of these beggar weddings in mind. Their sharp condemnation of the new marriage customs reflects this point of view, which derives especially from the experiences of crisis and famine years. The passage of time and our historical awareness permit us to place the personal-human aspect in the foreground. In so doing, not only can we illuminate more clearly the change in ways of life, but in contrast to the sources, we have to assess differently and more positively these pathbreaking innovations.

To begin with, it must be emphasized that it is not industrialization that altered the customs and usages of this great passage in life, matrimony. Such an interpretation would imply a purely materialistic conception of history that we cannot share. Industrialization simply gave to a broad layer of the rural population the material possibility of taking over new ways of life from other groups or of developing these for itself. With industrialization these people could individualize courtship and marriage. This development must be viewed against a background of the larger Western tendency toward individualism, which got its decisive push in the late Renaissance and the Reformation. A transformation of the erotic consciousness is implicit in this development. A privileged layer of the urban bourgeoisie copies and takes over already developed forms of a courtly-aristocratic way of life. With the dissolution of the baroque unity of life, the erotic consciousness is isolated from this heightened universal context and secularized; imbued by Pietism with a new warmth, an ego-centered Eros arises. . . . In the first half of the nineteenth century, bourgeois love receives its outer and inner mold, which still today, dissolved and recast as the "dream boat" of romantic love, sings to us from every radio and record player. It is in this context, sketched here with a few catch words, that we must view the transformation . . . that was triggered by the availability of income from industry. Along with urban fashions and the luxurious tastes of the city, a spiritual-emotional attitude and its external manifestations penetrated the manufacturing population of the Zurich countryside.

Putting-out industry gave girls and boys the material prerequisites for marriage, and this possibility did away with any hesitation or fears that the young might have about knowing and getting to love each other. With no material considerations to stand in the way, one could yield to the attraction of the other sex. "The young lad," writes Johann Schulthess, "begins, as soon as he is confirmed—as though it were a veritable initiation ceremony—to steal after one or more girls." These maidens, however, the writer continues, "knowing that they cannot get a man any other way, open their chambers to these night boys and abandon themselves to the certain or uncertain hope that, in case of pregnancy, they will not be abandoned to shame." "This picture," protests Schulthess, is not "the fantasy of an ivory-tower scholar; oh no, it is drawn from life." Apparently he had unfortunately seen with his own eyes as a young boy many an example of this scandalous behavior, which had become much more serious and common in the four decades since; . . . . Schulthess refers to the inspection records of the rural pastors and cites from them a report: "The so-called practice of bundling [zu Licht gehen] gets to be looked upon as a right and a freedom, and to be considered as nothing sinful. Marriage is always the sequel of pregnancy."

Once again it would be wrong to see the form of courtship known as bundling—z'Licht go, as it is called in the Zurich countryside—as a product of the means of existence offered by putting-out industry. Bundling goes back to preindustrial times and arises essentially from the circumstances of small peasant and village life. Only, with the coming of home industry, bundling was taken over by a much larger population.

. . . .

The subject of births leads us to that of the external family structure, and to the problem of the increase in population.

The economists of the nineteenth century were not the first to note and to try to explain this increase. Already in the eighteenth century concerned men, conscious of their responsibility, were writing articles on the subject. People everywhere were aware that this striking surplus of births was a direct consequence of industrialization. We have already heard the opinion of Salomon Schinz that industrial earnings "planted," as it were, the multitudes in the mountains. Johann Schulthess speaks of a "torrent of people" and cites the expression of a deceased pastor: "These people came with cotton and must die with it." Even more vivid is the observation of a rich peasant and village official with whom Uli Brägger conversed in 1793: "The cotton industry, like a foul pile of dung, has produced and given birth to all this vermin, the crawling and proud beggar pack." Behind all these formulations stood the same observation: the putting-out industry had changed the conditions of existence in the Zurich countryside.

[Braun then offers statistics showing that an industrialized rural commune like Wald saw its population increase almost fivefold from 1634 to 1792, whereas the major urban center of Zurich went only from 9,122 to 10,579 in the period 1671–1769; similarly, the rural district of Hinwil actually had in 1836 a population density almost equal to that of Zurich.]

. . . .

We have posed here the double question of the external structure of the family and its inner cohesion. The fact of a surplus of births and an increase in population does not mean that marriages were becoming more fecund. . . . The industrial population cannot be viewed here as a whole without distorting the picture. We must start by making a distinction.

In those places where the industrial population was still able to keep something of its peasant holdings or—especially true for the Highlands —was acquiring new land, other circumstances prevailed than among the landless cottage workers. It is striking how property in the soil works to the preservation of kinship ties even in putting-out circles. The practice of *Rastgeben* [allowances from children to parents] could not assume among propertied families those forms that we shall study in the next section in regard to the families of landless cottage workers. Wherever a mountain peasantry established itself on the basis of industrial earnings, the children were obliged to devote their efforts to the common economy. They could not abdicate the task of earning the costs of the property by spinning and weaving. How much of this customary compulsion determined the fate of the daughters, especially, is known to us from the accounts of an old woman silk weaver. She reports that her family counted on her earnings as a matter of course. "Only wait until your daughter grows up," the neighbor said to her father, "then you can put some money aside." Naturally one gave up the money earned in this way to the family and used it for the common household or those of the brothers. The sister of the informant wove at home until her fortieth year, putting all her earnings into the common pot. In such a familial economic unit, the bonds between parents and children, determined as they were by material forces, were strong, and no restrictions were placed on the fecundity of a marriage. Children, especially daughters, were desired. The abovementioned neighbor of our informant had himself seven daughters.

. . . .

If then we are justified in expecting from propertied marriage at the least a stable rate of fertility, this is not true for the marriages of landless cottage workers. Children were not at all welcome in such circles, even though they were already able to defray their own upkeep at a tender age. The parents were not unhappy to see them leave and board out with strangers. As hard and "inhuman" as we may find this today, the parents were also not unhappy to see their children die. When Uli Brägger was cured of a dangerous illness, his father said to him: "God has heard your entreaties. . . . I, however, I'm willing to admit, did not think as you did, Uli, and would have considered myself and you fortunate if you had passed away." Johann Schulthess writes: "Hence so many parents who not only think about it, but wish loudly and openly for the death of their children. You can hear —I'm speaking now as a witness—a needy woman murmur against heaven because a child of a well-to-do neighbor has died: "I am not so lucky," she says. "If one of my children fell off the bench, instead of his breaking his neck, two of them would spring up in his place." And another woman, a gleaner, walking next to her pastor in the street and holding the hand of a lively child hardly recovered from the pox, says without shame in front of both of them: "Oh, if it had only died of the pox!"

This attitude toward offspring and child was determined on the one hand by purely external motives. The small child keeps the mother from her work. But for her, time is money. Once the child grows up and can pay for his own upkeep, it enters into the customary *Rast* [allowance] relationship. On the other hand, the inconceivably bad housing also played a role. The sharp increase in population, combined with local prohibition on construction, gave rise to a housing situation in which any increase in the size of the household necessarily had the effect of an unbearable burden.

. . . .

We emphasized above that in those families which are still firmly rooted in their own soil and property, the allowance system is not found. The children turn their earnings as a matter of course over to the economic unit. The maintenance of the property has priority over individual happiness. Thus the sister of the abovementioned informant, who lived in the house until her fortieth year, had no savings of her own.

As soon as this spiritual and emotional tie to the family property and the soil changes, forms of the allowance system necessarily develop. Unquestionably, such a tendency becomes stronger with the growth of industrialization. The relationship of cause and effect cannot, however, be established in general terms, but depends in each case on the particular circumstances. Johann Conrad Nüscheler provides us with a very instructive example. On inquiring about the reason for unused and neglected holdings, he "generally" received the following answer: "My wife and I are getting old. We can't work so much as before. We also have three children, two of whom pay us each week an allowance of 30 Batzen [a small coin]. Only the one daughter stills helps us in our work. We work only as much as we can and have to, and eke out our living with what the two other children give us. It would be very hard for us to find workers and day laborers, or to support a boy and a maid: board and wages are much too high. Thank God, we can make out right well with what the children give us." The example shows how far the process had developed in the course of a generation. For not only have the children lost their interest in their peasant holding, but in the resignation of the parents one can see that the pride of the peasant in his own land has disappeared. The source throws light on the inner composition of the family. The strongest ties to parents and farm are those of the daughter who is still working in the enterprise. The other children have merely an allowance relationship, that is, they pay their 30 Batzen maintenance and no longer have any obligation to work. They have become boarders in their own family. If, in this family, still peasant, though to be sure only partially so, the changes have been able to proceed so far in a generation, we shall not be surprised by the development of the

allowance system among those people who have had no land or
property for generations. . . . In these circles it is not only usual for
the children to pay their parents their weekly allowance "and to think
that they have bought thereby complete independence," but even
these loosest of family ties are broken, and the children go out and
board in the homes of strangers.

. . . .

The social consequences of the allowance system are obvious:
although the rules on construction and the lack of freedom of
movement hold the industrial family unit together in a physical sense,
the inner cohesion of the family is weakened. One is tempted to
blame all these nuisances on industrialization, for it brings, along
with its demands for labor, the material possibility of loosening
family ties. And yet one must keep in mind where these people had
to seek their bread before industrialization. If the father is earning
his and his family's upkeep in Swabia, the daughter is working as a
domestic in Zurich, the oldest son is fighting in Dalmatia, and the
mother, with the rest of the family, is spinning in Fischenthal, one
can hardly speak of an inner and outer family togetherness. That was
the fate of poor, small peasant families: day workers, laborers, and
tolerated squatters. How about the propertied ones? Either those
children who had no inheritance rights gave up the idea of founding
a family and remained as valets and maids on the farm, or they were
compelled to leave and make their fortune elsewhere. The critics
of the eighteenth and also the twentieth century find it easy to forget these aspects of preindustrial peasant life, because those afflicted
by them live out their lives at a distance—out of sight, out of mind.
These critics place only a negative value on the social consequences
of industrialization and sing the praises of peaceful rural life. That
many were enabled for the first time by industrialization to remain
in their homeland—that they do not want to see. For all that, however, the [unfavorable] social consequences of the allowance system
are in no way to be gainsaid or depreciated. We are simply trying
here to view fairly the light and dark sides of the picture.

JOSIAH WEDGWOOD AND FACTORY DISCIPLINE *

Neil McKendrick †

. . . .

Like Soho, Cromford and Coalbrookdale, Etruria served as a model to its own industry.[1] It ushered in the factory system and the age of industrialization to the Potteries. But in basing his works on the division of labour Wedgwood merely followed and speeded up a process already in motion. In the middle of the eighteenth century the whole of the Potteries, together with industry in general, was moving towards greater specialization. Vital technical changes were altering the whole economic organization of the Staffordshire pot-banks. The family craftsman stage had already given way to the master potter with his journeymen and apprentices recruited from outside the family, and this in turn was becoming inadequate to deal with the growing complexity of potting production.[2] New wares demanded new techniques: moulded ware required specialized block cutters, flat and hollow ware pressers, and casters. Specialization bred further improvement and variety: old shapes were reformed and old methods refined; new bodies were discovered, new glazes evolved, and new clays imported. Potters of limited means and restricted ambition

---

* Reprinted in abridged form from *The Historical Journal*, **IV** (1961), pp. 30–55. Used by permission of the author.

† Neil McKendrick is a Fellow of Gonville and Caius College, Cambridge University. He is currently preparing a history of Josiah Wedgwood.

[1] [Soho, Cromford, Coalbrookdale, and Etruria were respectively the sites of the Boulton-Watt engine works, Arkwright's first cotton mill, the Darby iron foundry (where in 1709, iron was first smelted successfully with coal), and Wedgwood's porcelain factory.]

[2] For some discussion of the economic development of the Potteries, cf. R. T. Ely, *Studies in the Evolution of Industrial Society* (1903), chs. i–iii, and the work of John Thomas: "The Economic Development of the North Staffordshire Potteries since 1730, with special reference to the Industrial Revolution", an unpublished Ph.D. thesis presented to London University in 1934; "The Pottery Industry and the Industrial Revolution", *Econ. Hist.* (supplement to the *Econ. J.*), III (1937), 399–414; and "Pottery in England in the Industrial Revolution", *J. R. Soc. Arts*, LXXXIV (1936), 521–46.

began to find the range of products too large to handle, and the effort of reorganization too great to accept. For not only were new wares required to compete for the growing market, but new methods of production were needed to exploit this increasing demand. The simple pot-bank was no longer adequate.

Wedgwood refused to be deterred by the difficulties of reorganization. Occasionally when things were going badly, he might 'almost envy many of my Brethren for the simplicity of their work, & the ease with which they can command Plates, Dishes & Chamberpots to be made from one years end to another', but he was determined to improve *his* methods of production. He was convinced from the outset that the only efficient means were the division of labour and the separation of different processes. Between 1767 and 1769 the plans for the layout of Etruria changed frequently, but Wedgwood never contemplated abandoning 'the scheme of keeping each workshop separate, which I have much set my heart on'. The 'Useful Works' and the 'Ornamental Works' were to be kept completely apart, each with their own kilns and their own sets of hands. At this stage he planned 'five portions', each to house a major stage in the production of earthenware. It was the plan that all potters would eventually follow. For like his fictional descendant, Henry Mynors, he 'designed the Works with a view to the strictest economy of labour. The various shops were so arranged that in the course of its metamorphosis the clay travelled naturally in a circle from the ship house by the canal to the packing house by the canal: there was no carrying to and fro.' [3]

He adopted the same system in planning the enamel works at Greek Street. His designs aimed at a conveyor belt progress through the works: the kiln room succeeded the painting room, the account room the kiln room, and the ware room the account room, so that there was a smooth progression from the ware being painted, to being fired, to being entered into the books, to being stored. Yet each process remained quite separate. He organized his men on the same basis, for he believed that 'the same hands cannot make *fine* & *coarse—expensive* & *cheap articles* so as to turn to any good account to the Master'. The 'fine figure Painters are another ord(e)r of beings' compared with the common 'flower painters' and must be treated accordingly—paid higher wages, set to work in a different workshop, and encouraged to specialize. His workmen were not allowed to

[3] Arnold Bennett, *Anna of the Five Towns* (London, 1902; reprinted 1904), p. 116.

wander at will from one task to another as the workmen did in the pre-Wedgwood potteries. They were trained to one particular task and they had to stick to it. Wedgwood felt that this was the only way to improve the quality of the ware—'We are preparing some hands to work at red & black . . . (ware) . . . *constantly* & *then we shall make them good,* there is no such thing as making now & then a few of any article to have them tolerable.'

. . . This system had its drawbacks for the workmen. For although they were paid higher wages for their expertise, they were more vulnerable to changing demand and fluctuations in the market. When the fashionable world turned against gilding for instance, Wedgwood wrote, 'Gold, the most precious of all metals is absolutely kicked out of doors, & our poor Gilders I believe must follow it.' [4] Such violent changes in taste were fortunately rare and, in a world of expanding markets, the potter in general gained from specialization. Certainly the quality of the pottery improved, and that was Wedgwood's major consideration.

The analysis of workers at Etruria drawn up by Alexander Chisholm, Wedgwood's secretary and amanuensis, in the early 1790's, shows to what extent the division of labour had been developed. . . . Out of the 278 men, women and children that Wedgwood employed in June 1790, only five had no specified post. These five were listed simply as 'Odd men', the lowest in the hierarchy and the first to go in bad times. The rest were specialists. However humble their task they did it constantly, and therefore they did it well. To pretend as some do that the division of labour destroyed skill is to deny the superiority of Wedgwood's products over his rivals, and to sentimentalize the crude Staffordshire salt glaze of his predecessors. Division of labour did not destroy skill: it limited its field of expression to a particular task, but within those limits it increased it. . . .

This great change in the organization of labour had not occurred without difficulty. Having designed his system, Wedgwood had to train men to fit it, and to regiment them to exploit its potentialities. His twin task was, in his own words, first, 'to make *Artists* . . . (of) . . . mere *men*', and second, to 'make such *machines* of the *Men* as cannot err'.

His lack of trained painters and modellers was immediately

---

[4] For the importance of taste and fashion in production, cf. Neil McKendrick, 'Josiah Wedgwood: An Eighteenth Century Entrepreneur in Salesmanship and Marketing Technique', *Econ. Hist. Rev.* XII, no. 3 (1960), 408–33.

apparent. Such was his need that he was forced to advertise for and employ men whose only experience was painting 'Coaches, Fans, (or) Waiters' and to recruit those cast off by Derby, Worcester and Bow.[5] But these were only temporary measures. Wedgwood was convinced that

few hands can be got to paint . . . in the style we want them. I may add, nor any other work we do. *We must make them.* There is no other way. We have stepped forward beyond the other manufacturers & we must be content to train up hands to suit our purpose. . . .

He lost no time himself: women were trained to simple tasks like bordering, and old hands began a second apprenticeship. Before long a *'new made* flower painter' was on his way to London, and within a month 'two more recruits' set out on their long walk to the capital. The challenge clearly appealed to Wedgwood, and he constantly spurred on Bentley with the promise of 'Glory and honour', writing 'It is *hard,* but then it is *glorious* to conquer so great an Empire with raw, undisciplin'd recruits. What merit must the General have who achieves such wonders under such disadvantageous circumstances' . . .

By this time, however, Wedgwood had taken more positive action to meet the shortage. He realized that by retraining old hands he could solve only his immediate problems. For these workers, recruited from the rest of the pottery, were too ingrained in their ways to become first-rate painters and modellers. They grumbled at the new standards that Wedgwood set and accepted with reluctance the new techniques he wished them to master. He wrote to Bentley in exasperation,

We have now got thirty hands here, but I have much ado to keep the new ones quiet—some will not work in Black. Others say they shall never learn this new business, & want to be releas'd to make Terrines & sa(uce) boats again. I do not know what I shall do with them, we have too many *fresh* hands to take in at once, though we have business enough for them, if they knew how, or wo(ul)d have the patience to learn to do it, but they do not seem to relish the thoughts of a second apprenticeship.

Gradually he moulded them to his methods, but they were never more

[5] He only accepted such men because of strict necessity. He feared both the loss of secrets and the introduction of lax methods. Later he was very loath to accept such men, writing to Bentley on 8 Jan. 1775 (WMSS. E. 18582–25): 'No—I shall not ingag(e) the Man from Derby.—We have a very good sett of hands, & *I shall be very careful not to take in a rotten Sheep if I can avoid it.'* (My italics.)

than adequate. To achieve the perfection he demanded he had to train his workmen from youth.

He had of course always taken in apprentices in the conventional potting crafts. But something more than this was needed to meet his special requirements. He needed artists as well as craftsmen and there were 'none ready made'. As always his ambition and imagination were equal to the challenge, and he wrote,

I have a *Waking notion* haunts me very much of late which is the beginning a regular drawing, & modeling school to train up Artists for ourselves. I wo(ul)d pick up some likely boys of about 12 years old & take them apprentice 'till they are twenty or twenty one & set them to drawing & when you wanted any hands we could draft them out of this school. The Paintings upon these vases are from W & B school—so it may be s(ai)d 1000 years hence.

With the advice of visiting artists like George Stubbs and the coaching of George Barrett and Henry Webber, this apprenticeship in the arts flourished. It produced many skilful artists and occasionally the brilliant modeller, such as William Hackwood, who designed some of Wedgwood's most famous pieces.

It was a slow process, however, and Wedgwood often wished to supplement it. He did so by his occasional use of the highly paid artist, already accomplished in other fields. Wedgwood was not the first manufacturer to employ famous artists. The charming nudes of François Boucher frolicked across the tapestries produced at Beauvais as early as the 1740's; Falconet's figures were reproduced in biscuit porcelain in the 1750's; whilst Dodin's *putti* gambolled on Vincennes vases in the same decade, and Redouté's roses flowered on Sèvres soon after. But Wedgwood was one of the first scientific industrialists in England to seek the co-operation of serious artists in large-scale industrial production.[6]

. . . .

His great need in his factory, however, was for skilled hands at a lower level—men who could reproduce and adapt the original designs of the artists. Wedgwood had to curb his impatience for these and wait for the results of his drawing school, for he refused to disrupt his factory discipline with the pretensions of the famous,

[6] It is worth remembering, too, that unlike Meissen, Vincennes, and Sèvres, Wedgwood had to make a profit to survive. He did not receive like them the royal subsidies that made their patronage of artists possible and cushioned them against financial losses.

writing, 'Oh! for a dozen good & *humble* modelers at Etruria for a couple of months. What creations, renovations, & generations should we make! Well—fair & softly, we must proceed with our own natural forces, for I will have no *fine* modelers here, though I seem to wish for them, they would corrupt, & ruin us all.'

His training of his own workmen never lapsed and in 1790 nearly 25 per cent of his workmen were apprentices. Many of them were girls. For in the 1770's he had gone to great expense and infinite trouble to train and introduce girls into his works. He paid the men more to persuade them to accept female apprentices; he soothed their *amour-propre* with flattery; and countered their objections with a show of indignant rage. They proved a difficult and expensive introduction, but when in 1779 they could finally 'be reckon'd complete hands' their cheap labour began to pay dividends.

Moreover, like all his apprentices they were trained to his own high standards, they were steady, remorseless and efficient. Without the pretensions of the famous, the dangers of the imported, or the careless habits of the older generations, these young potters were Wedgwood's contribution to the tradition of the skilled artisan of the nineteenth century. He was by no means unique. Brindley had transformed miners and common labourers into experienced tunnellers; Watt had found millwrights and left skilled engineers; Arkwright had begun with clock-makers and finished with trained machinists and George Stephenson was to turn the humble pitmen of Tyneside into the famed architects of the railway world.[7] In the same way, Wedgwood had taken semi-skilled potters and left specialist craftsmen, or as he put it 'made Artists' of 'mere men'.

Wedgwood had not only to train a new generation of skilled potters, he had also to mould these workers to the needs of his factory system. It was not an easy task, for he had centuries of local tradition to oppose him. The potters had enjoyed their independence too long to take kindly to the rules which Wedgwood attempted to enforce—the punctuality, the constant attendance, the fixed hours, the scrupulous standards of care and cleanliness, the avoidance of waste, the ban on drinking. They did not surrender easily. The stoppages for a wake or a fair or a three-day drinking spree were an accepted part of the potter's life—and they proved the most difficult to uproot. When they did work, they worked by rule of thumb; their methods of production were careless and uneconomical; and their

---

[7] T. S. Ashton, *The Industrial Revolution 1760–1830* (London, 1949), 120–21, and L. T. C. Rolt, *George and Robert Stephenson* (London, 1960), 76.

working arrangements arbitrary, slipshod and unscientific. For they regarded the dirt, the inefficiency and the inevitable waste, which their methods involved, as the natural companions to pot-making.

All of these problems were accentuated by the changes that had taken place in the Potteries. For in the development from the simple pot bank to the complex factory, the natural source of authority—that of the master potter—was lost, or at least greatly diminished by the growth in numbers. The discipline of one man was no longer adequate. To handle ten men had presented no great problem to the potter who worked in the same room, who shared the same interests, and who administered a rough and ready justice on the spot. 'But to keep 150 hands of various professions, & more various tempers & dispositions, in *tolerable* order' was a more difficult task. Wedgwood himself could cope with it. There can be little doubt of his authority. The impact on his workmen of his almost brutal face—stern even when composed by a Hackwood or portrayed by the grace of a Reynolds—was clear even to himself: 'my name has been made such a scarecrow to them, that the poor fellows are frighten'd out of their wits when they hear of Mr W. coming to town, & I perceive upon our first meeting they look as if they saw the D(evi)l'. . . .

Wedgwood, however, had a host of other business and was forced with increasing frequency to leave them 'without any head to look after them'. To solve these problems Wedgwood had to seek substitutes for his own authority, and to dispense his discipline through written rules and regulations.

Effective substitutes proved difficult to find. There was no tradition of a foreman or managerial class, for there had previously been little necessity for it. Merely to promote old hands was not enough—too often they connived at faults, which familiarity had robbed of significance, and too easily lapsed into irregularity as soon as they were left unsupervised. As Wedgwood wrote of one promoted hand, 'Daniel does pretty well when at work, & I am here every day, but he often leaves the works, & drinks two or three days together, & has no taste to direct at any time'. This position was never adequately filled until his nephew, Thomas Byerley, and his sons were able to share some of the burden of decision and responsibility. The works would usually tick over satisfactorily in his absence but all new problems were shelved and the rebellious took the opportunity to prepare their grievances. When he was away for a fortnight—on his honeymoon—deliveries stopped altogether, and even in 1772 he returned to find 'every species of business that has any puzzle in it &

could possibly be delay'd, has been put off to greet my arrival here, &
every day I have battles of various kinds, & orders to fight my way
thro'. . . . His temporary solution was to rely on an overseer, or
inspector, or superintendent, or looker-over in each workshop, rather
than one man in charge of the whole works. Wedgwood had solved
his problem by dividing the responsibility and reintroducing the unit
of the old pot bank, with 'one steady man' to each process. They
were reinforced by the 'Clerk of the Manufactory', the 'Clerk of
Weights & Measures', the porter, and general inspectors to 'look after
the men & wages'. This system succeeded where individuals bearing
the whole responsibility had failed. It was a technique that Wedgwood repeated in the supervision of canals when he suggested 'Walking Surveyors' who 'were . . . to be the Ears & Eyes for the
Committee'.

   With Bentley's death in 1780, Josiah's problems grew more acute.[8]
Inevitably he would have to divide his time between London and
Etruria, and more often leave his workers to their own devices. He
had to bolster up the authority of his 'foremen'. His solution—for
surely it cannot be coincidence—lay in the 'Potters' Instructions' of 1780
and 'the regulations and rules made for this manufactory more than
30 years back' which were written down by R. Rhead, in 1810. They
cover every aspect of factory discipline. Containing a remarkably
detailed knowledge of every workshop and every process, the Instructions recognize all the minor techniques, the tricks and petty
evasions of the idle workman. In this way Wedgwood armed his
overseers with his experience, his knowledge of prevalent faults and
his remedies. They also provided clear instructions on how 'to show
marks of approbation' to the skilful and the punctual and how 'to
reprimand those more slovenly & careless'.

   One of the major problems was to ensure prompt and regular
attendance at the works. As was usual Wedgwood set himself off
from the rest of the potters by introducing the bell. One of his early
factories was known in fact as the Bell Works, because the workmen
were summoned by ringing a bell instead of blowing a horn as was
the custom in the district. Moreover, Wedgwood laid down precise
times when it should be rung—the first warning at 5.45 or a '¼ of
an hour before (the men) can see to work', again at 8.30 for breakfast,
at nine to recall them and so on until 'the last bell when they can no

   [8] [Thomas Bentley was Wedgwood's partner from 1769. See Ralph M. Hower,
"The Wedgwoods—Ten Generations of Potters," *Journ. of Econ. and Business
History,* **IV** (1932), pp. 288-290.]

longer see'. He did not rely on the bell alone. He employed a 'Clerk of the Manufactory' who was

> to be at the works the first in the morning, & settle the people to their business as they come in—to encourage those who come regularly to their time, letting them know that their regularity is properly noticed, & distinguishing them by repeated marks of approbation, from the less orderly part of the work people by *presents or other marks suitable to their age &c.* Those who come later than the hour appointed should be noticed, and if after repeated marks of disapprobation they do not come in due time, an account of the time they are deficient in should be taken, & *so much of their wages stopt* as the time comes to. . . .

In doing this he was doing no more than other manufacturers—Arkwright rewarded his most deserving workers with 'distinguishing dresses . . . which excites great emulation', and Ambrose Crowley fixed fines for lateness.[9] But Wedgwood's further ideas to encourage punctuality and prevent loss of working time seem to be without equal.

For in his Commonplace Book, he also outlined a scheme which can be compared only with a primitive clocking-in system. He wrote,

> To save the trouble of the porters going round, tickets may perhaps be used, in the following manner—Let some sheets of pasteboard paper be printed with the names of all the work people, and the names cut off, about the size of half a card. Let each person take two of these tickets with him when he leaves work every evening; one of which he is to deliver into a box when he goes through the lodge in the morning, and the other when he returns from dinner. The porter then, instead of going round the works in the morning, looks over these tickets only; & if he finds any deficiency, goes to such places only where the deficiency appears. If the persons have neglected or refused to deliver their tickets on going through, they are to to be admonished the first time, the second time to pay a small fine to the poors box. . . . It will be necessary to have divisions for the tickets in alphabetic order, for the greater facility of giving them out.

To speed up this process, he considered further refinements, and proposed a list of 'all the names in alphabetic order on a board hung up in the lodge' to be marked by the porter with different coloured chalks to record the time of arrivals. He reinforced this system and prevented its abuse by imposing a fine of 2s. on 'any workman scaling the walls or Gates', and a similar 'forfeit' on 'any workman forseing

---

[9] [Sir Ambrose Crowley (1658–1713) was probably the greatest English ironmaster of his day. See Michael W. Flinn, *Men of Iron: The Crowleys in the Early Iron Industry* (Edinburgh, 1962).]

(*sic*) their way through the lodge after the time alowed (*sic*) by the Master'. Wedgwood's intentions were clear from his factory. The most prominent feature of Etruria was the bell, the next—the clock. To judge from his workers' wage-sheets, on which were marked the time of arrival, of departure and the time they had for meals, his methods were fully successful. His workmen even organized a pay demand outside the main gates, promptly at half-past six.

. . . .

His attention to cleanliness and the avoidance of waste was equally scrupulous. Apart from his fines—'any workman leaveing a fire in there (*sic*) rooms at night forfits 2s. 6d' and 'any workman leaveing there scraps in there rooms so as to get dirty forfits 2s.'—he introduced scales and a clerk to operate them. As early as 1769, he wrote to Bentley,

I am often giving my people lessons upon the loss of Clay, & with it the loss of credit in making heavy ware, but all will not do, I have bo(ugh)t them half a doz. pair(s) of scales, but there seems one thing want(in)g still which I propose to have soon—*A Clerk of weight & measures,* whose constant business it shall be to weigh the goods as they are got up—he will save me three times his wages in *Clay,* & ten times as much in *Credit.* The first clever fellow I can spare shall certainly be set down to this business.

This clerk's duties rapidly grew. After weighing the clay he was 'to lay it up with as much cleanness as if it was intended for food'. He had further to supervise the scraping, the sponging, the breaking open and the careful examining of the clay 'for red or yellow veins & other foulnesses'. Each process must take place on a separate bench, cleaned beforehand and set 'before a good light'. It is almost needless to say that the *utmost cleanness* should be observed thro' out the whole slip & clay house—the floors kept clean—& (even) *the avenues leading to the slip & clay houses* sho^d be *kept clean likewise.* And in sumer (*sic*) time when it is dusty, watered likewise.' To defeat evasion the clerk was to pay 'check visits irregularly' and search for dirt when he was least expected.

Every aspect of the potter's trade was covered in his instructions: there were separate directions for the throwers, the handlers, the pressers, the finishers and the dishmakers; and there were equally detailed comments on every object made—from the need to check the number of holes in the grate of a teapot spout to the need for heavy bases for salt cellars. All had to be checked by the overseer or Clerk of the Manufactory. He had to watch that the clays were not mixed 'soft & hard all together promiscuously', he had to ensure that the saggars were completely dry, for even a little damp could cover the glazed ware 'with large air bubbles like pustules of the small pox'; he had to restrict the too frequent use of the sponge which could mark the glaze 'like the sweep of a broom on a sanded floor'; he had to make sure that the turners left 'the surface free of all blemishes, wrinkles, scratches &c. like a fine piece of uniformly polished marble'; and finally he must examine the lawns '2 or 3 times a day', for if neglected 'the mishcief (sic) will be very extensive'. In addition, there were constant exhortations to the clerk himself. Stern warnings that 'this examination should never be omitted' were backed up by reminders that 'the clerk must see with his own eyes that it is done, at least till he has by experience a well grounded assurance of . . . punctuality. He may then make his check visits fewer but never altogether neglect them.' He must not be entirely critical, however, for to the virtuous 'he should no more forget to show marks of his approbation than to reprimand those more slovenly and careless'.

Wedgwood's reaction to carelessness was more violent. The famous story of Wedgwood stumping through his works, smashing sub-standard pots and chalking on the bench 'this won't do for Josiah Wedgwood', is supported by the facts at least as far as the smashing. Legend alone provides the chalk. But for once legend needs no excuse. It fits the man, it fits his character and what little evidence there is supports it. In 1773 he wrote 'The Argyles . . . are not clever, I have broke 4 or 5 doz that I found finish'd here this morning, & ord^d some improvements'; in 1779 he wrote, 'We cannot master Achilles. I have had him demolished . . . more than once' and he invariably smashed ware which he said would 'do us no credit'. . . .

To supplement his particular rules concerning punctuality, cleanliness and avoidance of waste and error, he had a list of forfeits of a more general nature. Wedgwood was never one to leave loopholes in his discipline if he could avoid it, and none of his workmen could complain that the rules were not clear. They read, apart from those already quoted, 'any person seen throwing within the yard of this manufactory to forfit 2s. 6d.', 'any workman strikeing or otherwise abuseing an overlooker to loose his or there place', 'any workman conveying Ale or Licquor into the manufactory in working hours forfits 2s.', 'any person writeing obseen or other writeing upon the walls either within or without the works forfits for every offence 2s. 6d.', 'any person playing at fives against any of the walls where there are windows forfits 2s.' These were not light fines. When one remembers that the average workman's wage was approximately one-twentieth of his twentieth-century equivalent, the true impact of these fines can be realized. A forfeit of 2s. 6d. was—again very approximately—equivalent to a fine of £2. 10s. to a workman today. It is unlikely that they were often ignored.

Moreover, the promiscuity and immorality that Arnold Bennett describes as the commonplace of the Staffordshire pot bank had little chance to flourish in Wedgwood's factory. The reason was not so much morality as a desire for efficiency. When Bentley's servants frolicked below stairs, Wedgwood wrote tolerantly and lightheartedly 'the Kitchen is always more than a match for the Parlour where the utmost vigilance takes place—and with you who as well as myself, rejoice that art does not yet triumph over nature universally, there would be little hope of succeeding in any attempts against such natural connections'. . . . In his works, however, such activities were regarded in a very different light. Gone was the happy tolerance: the offending housekeeper was removed '& if any of our people will keep up such connections with her as you do not approve of I wo^d remove them too'.

His rules, however, were not for his benefit alone. There were, for example, strict precautions 'taken to avoid the pernicious effects of lead' poisoning. And his rules for dippers show his usual attention to detail: 'The dipping rooms to be cleaned out with a mop *never* brushed', 'A pail of water with soap and a towel & a brush for the nails to be always at hand', 'No one to be allowed to eat in the dipping room', 'The men and the boys to have an upper dress to throw off when they leave the room, for instance a sort of smock frock with long sleeves & open behind would be convenient', 'Some ware (such) as tiles require to have part of the surface freed from the glaze, this should be done with a sponge, & *not as now* by brushing when dry'. Such prophylactics are still the basis of industrial hygiene in the potteries today.

Yet for all this, according to Ashton 'the second generation of employers—such as the younger Boulton, Watt, Wedgwood, or Crawshay—was perhaps more alive than the first to the losses that might arise from the irregularity or carelessness on the part of labour'.[10] It is difficult to believe that this was true of the Wedgwoods. Josiah employed all the new methods of administration, the new incentives, and new discipline that Ashton attributes to his successors. 'Men

[10] [T. S. Ashton, *The Industrial Revolution,* p. 123. Richard Crawshay, active toward the end of the eighteenth century, was known in his time as the "Iron King." See J. P. Addis, *The Crawshay Dynasty: A Study in Industrial Organisation and Development, 1765–1867* (Cardiff, 1957).]

trained in the concern were appointed as managers and foremen; piecerates and bonus schemes were introduced to stimulate effort; fines were imposed for drunkenness, sloth, and gaming.' Admittedly some he found difficult to apply, but no one was 'more alive' to their need.

In only one thing did he fail almost completely—the control of wakes and fairs. He had little defence against their attraction, and production was interrupted with ironic regularity every summer. In 1771 he wrote, 'I should have sent you some good black ones this week, *if it had not been Stoke Wake*', and in 1772 he apologized for slow delivery, saying, 'the Men have gone madding after these Wakes's so that we could get little done'. . . . It was only slowly that the passion for wakes died—strangled by the joint efforts of the manufacturers, the methodists, and the Society for the Suppression of Vice.

But if Wedgwood was unable to uproot their annual bacchanalia, he purged his workers of most of their other industrial faults. By his own persistence, by an unfailing attention to detail, by founding, if not creating, the traditions of a foreman class and equipping it with rules and regulations, he transformed a collection of what in 1765 he called, 'dilatory drunken, idle, worthless workmen', into what ten years later he allowed to be, 'a very good sett of hands'. He never fully achieved the reformation he had hoped for. He never made 'such *Machines* of the *Men* as cannot Err', but he certainly produced a team of workmen who were cleaner, soberer, healthier, more careful, more punctual, more skilled and less wasteful than any other potter had produced before.

. . . .

In fact, although the discipline he imposed in his factory was a severe one, it was born of a desire to improve his workmen's lot. For Wedgwood was no mere Gradgrind. He moved in a society of liberal reformers [11]—men who read and gave him to read the works of Priestley, Price, Paine, Rousseau, Cartwright, Howard and Malthus. From these he formed his decided views of society. He saw it as it was—crude, filthy, incompetent and wasteful—and he wished to reform it. He saw men as improvable—even perfectable. Liberal but unsophisticated in his ideals he felt that his workmen should be disciplined for their own good, and offered security in return for obedience. He doubted his charges' ability to take their own decisions and as a substitute imposed his own massive authority.

[11] For a discussion of their attitudes, cf. Neil McKendrick, 'Wedgwood and his Friends', *Horizon*, I, 5 (1959), 88–97 and 128–30; and also J. Bronowski and Bruce Mazlish, *The Western Intellectual Tradition* (1960), ch. xviii.

The life he designed for his workmen was not an indulgent one. They were not to have the luxury of downing tools for a wake or a fair; nor of working for three days in order to drink for four. The cherished St. Monday was to be unfrocked, and all the gods of idleness and mindless enjoyment similarly banished. Time was the new idol—together with care, regularity and obedience. There can be no doubt that the workmen lost much of their old liberty, and their lives much of its old variety. For in the brave new world envisaged by Wedgwood and his friends there was little place for brothels, alehouses, cock-fighting and bull-baiting for the ease and amusement of his workmen. In their place there would be schools for their children, hospitals for their sick, homes for their orphans, and societies, libraries and institutions for themselves. For all there would be better food, better clothes, better houses, better roads and better transport. Their streets would be lit, their roads paved, their towns drained.

To achieve these ends, he demanded complete obedience, and complete submission. He also expected hard work. Accustomed to long hours and unremitting labour himself, he expected an effort of a similar nature from his workmen. Of his own industry and devotion there is ample evidence. His energy was remarkable and little daunted him. The lives of the engineers and the captains of industry are pockmarked with stories of endurance and application—Brunel working twenty hours a day for weeks on end on his Great Western Railway; [12] Whitbread sitting up four nights a week by his brewhouse copper and retiring only 'when the state of Boiling permitted'; [13] or Brindley fighting against diabetes for the last eight years of his life and giving advice even on his deathbed [14]—yet Wedgwood is worthy of comparison even with these Burleighs and Gladstones of industry. When his injured leg hampered his movements through his works and led to long periods of illness, he

[12] [L. T. C. Rolt, *Isambard Kingdom Brunel* (London, 1957), p. 75. "Between ourselves it is harder work than I like. I am rarely much under twenty hours a day at it." Isambard Brunel (1806–1859) was a leading railway and marine engineer who was responsible for a number of major advances in bridge and tunnel construction.]

[13] [*The House of Whitbread*, Vol. I. Samuel Whitbread (1720–1796) was "the leading porter brewer of his generation" and a model of the eighteenth-century entrepreneur. See Peter Mathias, *The Brewing Industry in England 1700–1830* (Cambridge, 1959).]

[14] [James Brindley (1716–1772), was the leading canal builder of his day. Among his major works were the Duke of Bridgewater's Worsley canal (1761), the Liverpool-Manchester (1767), and the Grand Trunk (begun 1766; completed 1777). See Samuel Smiles, *James Brindley and the Early Engineers* (London, 1864).]

coolly decided on amputation—facing the lack of anaesthetic and the great danger of gangrene with complete composure.

His amputation is the spectacular incident in his life—a moment of glamour—but it is unimpressive in the face of the burden of work that he carried. It is difficult to realize how much of the technical, clerical and managerial work the pioneers of industry dealt with. As late as the 1830's Brunel did everything in engineering the G.W.R. even down to choosing the variety of grass to grow alongside his rails: in the 1770's Wedgwood had to be in similar control of every detail. It was almost impossible to delegate responsibility. He had to decide everything from the shape of a coffee cup to the type of bricks for a new kiln— and he had little time in which to do it. In 1771 he wrote a long letter to Bentley discussing vital points of their sales policy whilst working in the lathe room and 'at such intervals as James could spare me'. There was no tradition of a managerial class to bear the burden of decision. The poor clerk class was as yet unborn. To deal with his correspondence he had to work before daybreak or after his workmen had left. 'I have stole a few moments from my wife this morning to converse a little with my friend 'till the world is wide awake for then I must of neces-sity mix with the bustling crowd. Everything is in the most violent agitation here'. . . . In 1769 his eyes became so bad that he was for-bidden to write by candlelight and had to use his wife as a scribe. He was told that his *sight* was at stake' and in January 1770 he wrote to Bentley of his preparations for blindness. 'I am often practising to *see* with my *fingers* & think I should make a tolerable proficient in that science for one who begins his studies so late in life, but shall make a wretched walker in the dark with a single leg.'

It was determination of this order which brought Wedgwood his great success, and it deeply influenced his attitude to his men. For he expected similar control and self-discipline from them. Therefore, although well disposed towards them, his attitude was always patriarchal and autocratic. He would correct, improve and direct for the common good; but he was not averse to punishment. He may have believed in liberty, but it was not the liberty to riot, and when in 1783 a riot broke out at Etruria he summoned the military and dispersed the mob by force. Two men were arrested, both of them convicted, and one of them subsequently hanged.

After this outbreak Wedgwood published a pamphlet called, *An Address to the Young Inhabitants of the Pottery,* pointing out the folly of using violence to redress social evils, and pleading with them

to use 'peaceable' means to cope with the present or any future discon-
tent. He went on to stress the temporary nature of the depression and
the great advance made by the Potters in the last generation.

Before I take my leave I would request you to ask your parents for a description of the country we inhabit when they first knew it; and they will tell
you, that the inhabitants bore all the signs of poverty to a much greater
degree than they do now. Their houses were miserable huts; the lands
poorly cultivated and yielded little of value for the food of man or beast,
and these disadvantages, with roads almost impassable, might be said to
have cut off our part of the country from the rest of the world, besides
not rendering it very comfortable to ourselves. Compare this picture which
I know to be a true one, with the present state of the same country. The
workmen earning nearly double their former wages—their houses mostly
new and comfortable, and the lands, roads and every other circumstance
bearing evident marks of the most pleasing and rapid improvements. From
whence and from what cause has this happy change taken place? You will
be beforehand with me in acknowledging a truth too evident to be denied
by any one. Industry has been the parent of this happy change—A well
directed and long continued series of industrious exertions, both in masters
and servants, has so changed for the better the face of our country, its
buildings, lands, roads, and not withstanding the present unfavourable
appearances, I must say the manner and deportment of its inhabitants too,
as to attract the notice and admiration of countries which had scarcely heard
of us before; and how far these improvements may still be carried by the
same laudable means which have brought us thus far, has been one of the
most pleasing contemplations of my life.

The argument followed familiar lines, but, for once, the facts were
accurate.

. . . .

There is ample evidence of this from sources other than Wedgwood's letters and speeches. Smiles wrote of the change, 'From a half-
savage, thinly-peopled district of some 7000 persons in 1760, partially
employed and ill remunerated, we find them increased, in the course
of some twenty-five years, to about treble the population, abundantly
employed, prosperous, and comfortable'.[15] Whilst John Wesley, who
was in a good position to judge since he had been stoned by the vicious
inhabitants of Burslem in 1760, wrote later, 'I returned to Burslem.
How is the whole face of the country changed in about twenty years!
Since which, inhabitants have continually flowed from every side.
Hence, the wilderness is literally become a fruitful field. Houses,

[15] Samuel Smiles, *Lives of the Engineers* (London, 1861), I, 448.

villages, towns have sprung up; and the country is not r
than the people.' [16]

Those who cherish the charms of peasant industry, :
the English workman's freedom. So, of course, did the wc
is nothing more frequent', wrote Defoe, 'than for an ___
work till he has got his pockets full of money, and then go and be idle
or perhaps drunk till 'tis all gone'. To change such habits was not easy:
nor was it always pleasant. It required exhortation, rewards and education to create a factory system. Wesley and the Sunday schools
taught the industrial virtues of diligence, thrift and regularity: Wedgwood's factory discipline—his bell, his embryonic clocking-in-system,
his rules and regulations—insisted on them. It is easy to condemn such
methods. But it would be ridiculous to deny their results. 'If the
workers of the eighteenth century had refused to conform to some
code of conduct when at work, there could have been no factory system,
and no such rise in output, and hence of the standard of life as was,
in fact, attained in the nineteenth century.' [17]

[16] *Ibid.*
[17] T. S. Ashton, *An Economic History of England: The 18th Century*
(London, 1955), p. 212.

INDUSTRIAL GROWTH AND INDUSTRIAL REVOLUTIONS *

D. C. Coleman †

The idea of the Industrial Revolution is one of the few items in the
private language of economic historians which has passed into common
parlance. By now *the* Industrial Revolution has surely earned its right,
along with ancient Greeks and early economists, to be called 'classical'.

* Reprinted from *Economica*, **XXIII**, n.s., February 1956, pp. 1–22. Used
by permission of *Economica* and the author.
† Donald C. Coleman is Reader in Economic History in the London School
of Economics, and Political Science and a specialist in the economic history of
England in the early modern period. Among his works are *The British Paper
Industry 1495–1860*; "Economic Problems and Policies," in the *New Cambridge
Modern History*, Vol. V; *The Ascendancy of France, 1648–1688*; and *Sir John
Banks, Baronet and Businessman*.

But as Sir George Clark pointed out some while ago,[1] other industrial revolutions are amongst us. In the writings of economic historians, revolutions abound. Leaving aside more than one commercial and agrarian 'revolution', the student of our subject is confronted with a succession of industrial revolutions. The late Bronze Age, the thirteenth century, the fifteenth century, the century from 1540 to 1640, the later seventeenth century and, passing over the classical industrial revolution, the late nineteenth and the early twentieth centuries—in all these periods it seems there may be observed industrial revolutions in the economic development of England alone. Other countries have their claimants, for example, Germany and Japan in the late nineteenth century.[2] At the present time, the possibilities of 'automatic factories' opened up by the development of electronic devices and their use in industrial control, has stimulated talk of an imminent 'second industrial revolution'. . . . This variety of uses of the term 'industrial revolution' can scarcely fail to be confusing. May it not be that the term has achieved its wide application at the expense of losing its true significance?

In the writing of economic history, three main forms of economic or technical 'revolutions' may be noted:

(i) The application to a particular industry. This frequently occurs in accounts of the growth of individual industries during the classical industrial revolution and is normally used to describe the introduction of a particular machine or technique which the writer regards as 'revolutionizing' the productive process in question and carrying with it comparably striking consequences, irrespective of what may or may not be happening in unrelated industries. Professor Carus-Wilson's 'Industrial Revolution' of the thirteenth century,[3] resting as it does on the mechanization of the process of fulling, comes within this category.

(ii) One stage more extensive than this use is the application of the term to particular branches of the economic activities of a society—industrial, commercial, agrarian and so forth. Thus the term 'industrial

---

[1] *The Idea of the Industrial Revolution,* David Murray Foundation Lecture, University of Glasgow (October 1952), Glasgow University Publication, XCV, 1953.

[2] Reference to the sources for most of these will be found in Clark, *op. cit.,* pp. 12–13. J. A. Schumpeter, *Business Cycles,* 2 vols., New York, 1939, contains various references to industrial revolutions in the late nineteenth and early twentieth centuries, e.g., pp. 397 and 753.

[3] E. M. Carus-Wilson, 'An Industrial Revolution of the Thirteenth Century', in *Econ. Hist. Rev.* XI, 1941; also reprinted in *Essays in Economic History* (ed. E. M. Carus-Wilson), London, 1954, and in E. M. Carus-Wilson, *Medieval Merchant Venturers,* London, 1954.

revolution' here means something which happens to industry as a whole, though not necessarily to other branches of the economy. It is implied in the O.E.D. definition: 'the rapid development *in industry* owing to the employment of machinery, which took place in England in the late eighteenth and early nineteenth centuries'. (My italics.)

(iii) The widest application is that to a national economy. Here the emphasis is not simply on the effect felt by an industry or by industry as a whole, but upon the consequences to the economy of a variety of changes in the sense that it moves rapidly into some new shape, normally that of the modern industrialized society. The classical English industrial revolution, as usually interpreted nowadays, is the prime example of this but the usage is increasingly extended to cover the same process experienced subsequently by other countries such as the U.S.A., Germany and Japan.

Variations have been played on these themes. One such variation is the building up of (iii) out of material used for (ii). Professor Nef's 'industrial revolution' [4] of the hundred years from 1540 to 1640 falls within this category. To some extent this implies an equating of the terms 'industrial revolution' and 'industrialization'.

The appearance in the subject of so many and such a variety of industrial revolutions raises the question of their identification. How are they to be recognized? Are they all of the same nature? The increasing use of quantitative methods in economic history presents us with industrial revolutions in statistical clothes. Is the concept something which can be measured, or at any rate detected, in appropriate statistical series? What is the relation of the concept, as used and developed by historians, to the studies by economists or statisticians of long-period industrial growth?

The aims of this article are as follows: to examine some of the implications of the use, by certain economic historians, of the term 'industrial revolution'; to relate these implications to the use of industrial growth curves; to examine the claim that the automatic factory is precipitating a second 'industrial revolution'; and finally, in an attempt to give some recognizable meaning to the term 'industrial revolution', to suggest certain very rough criteria for the continued employment of this overburdened phrase. In order to illustrate some of the problems involved in the relation between growth curves and industrial

---

[4] J. U. Nef: *The Rise of the British Coal Industry,* London, 1932, I, p. 165; 'The Progress of Technology and the Growth of Large-Scale Industry in Great Britain, 1540–1640', in *Econ. Hist. Rev.,* V, 1934 (reprinted in *Essays in Economic History*); and *War and Human Progress,* Cambridge, Mass., 1950.

revolutions, it is proposed to examine one industry in some detail and to suggest the possible applicability of the argument to other fields.

II

The one industry which it is proposed to examine in some detail is the English paper industry. A number of reasons combine to make this suitable for the purpose. It has a long history, spanning several centuries; it is an industry which peculiarly mirrors the growth of our industrial civilization, for its products find their way into extremely diverse and characteristic uses. Furthermore, it is especially useful for the purpose of examining the 'industrial revolution' in one industry and seeing it in quantitative terms, for it is possible to construct tolerably reliable series to cover the period from the early eighteenth century to the present day. And finally, its technical and economic history follows a course similar to that of other and better known industries.

Before examining the quantitative evidence of industrial growth which it offers, it is necessary to make a brief digression into some of the details of its technical and economic development.[5]

The techniques of paper making can be readily divided into a number of processes, just as can, for example, the techniques of the cloth industry. The history of technical progress in the latter is a history of mechanization stretching from the twelfth century (or earlier) to the early nineteenth century, in the approximate order: fulling, spinning, weaving, carding and combing, finishing, together with such comparatively early applications of industrial chemistry as the use of chlorine in bleaching, improvements in dyeing and the like. In paper making, technical progress followed a very similar course over roughly the same period of time. The main processes in the order in which they were effected (which is also the order in which they take place) are: raw material preparation, bleaching, forming the paper, drying and finishing. This includes the same early application of chemistry to industry in the shape of chlorine for bleaching. In addition, there followed a further crucial innovation in the industry, providing a new raw material—the discovery of wood pulp.

Before the later nineteenth century, the major raw materials for paper making were linen, and to a lesser extent cotton, rags. The pulping of the raw materials, which is the essential element in the first

---

[5] Further details of the paper industry can be found in my book, *The British Paper Industry, 1495–1860* (Clarendon Press, Oxford, 1958).

process, was originally carried out by hand, the rags being mixed with water and pounded. At what stage and where this process received its first mechanization, is not precisely known. The industry is said to have reached southern Europe by the eleventh and twelfth centuries, having come from China via the Middle East. It is claimed that in mid-twelfth century Spain a stamping mill, operated by water power, was at work macerating the rags in a series of large mortars. Such a mill was certainly in use at Nüremberg at the end of the fourteenth century, and thereafter various types of stamping mill, normally driven by water but sometimes by wind, formed a vital feature of the European paper mill until the eighteenth century. It then began to be replaced by an improved type of beating engine; this was at first driven by water power but later by steam. With many improvements and variations in detail, the preparation processes of washing, beating and pulping remain in principle the same today.[6]

The introduction of chlorine for rag bleaching need not detain us long. It came into use in the 1790's and was an obvious corollary to the similar results in the textile industry of Scheele's discovery.

Meanwhile, until the introduction of the paper-making machine in the first decade of the nineteenth century, the actual forming of the paper was everywhere a hand process. The parallel with the textile industry is striking. Just as water power was applied to fulling and much later to spinning, whilst weaving remained an entirely hand operation, so was power applied to rag preparation whilst the forming of a sheet was still done by hand. The linking of rag preparation to water power meant that paper mills were to be found on fast-running streams just as were so many mills, similarly powered, in other industries. To the striking technical resemblance between the fulling mill and the stamping mill there is added the tendency to determine location; indeed, when the paper industry was expanding in England from the sixteenth to the eighteenth centuries and the cloth industry geographically contracting, many former fulling mills were turned into paper mills.

By the end of the eighteenth century, then, paper making was a widespread European industry, Italy, France, Germany, Holland and Great Britain all having many mills. Water power and steam power (though the latter in only a very few places) had been applied to the first process and chemistry had made its mark on bleaching. In the first decade of the nineteenth century the paper-making machine was

[6] The making of wood pulp is, of course, an entirely different procedure, normally carried on in or near the forest areas.

introduced in the English industry. In the technical changes which it introduced, striking resemblances are again noticeable to the comparable changes in the textile industry in spinning and weaving. It was a straightforward mechanization of hand processes. In the hand process, the size of the sheet is normally limited to what can be conveniently manipulated by the paper maker; production is slow and labour highly skilled. The machine simply mechanized the whole procedure by forming the sheet on an endless wire gauze or mesh, thus allowing theoretically endless sheets of paper to be made. The modern machine is exactly the same in general principle though, of course with many improvements in detail and very much larger and faster.

Once the making had been mechanized, the mechanization of the drying and finishing processes followed rapidly. By the mid-nineteenth century, mechanization was complete. The output of the United Kingdom had multiplied about seventeen times since the mid-eighteenth century and the stage was set for the next crucial development.

During the 1850s and 1860s, the gales of the free trade movement had swept through the paper industry as elsewhere and removed both the excise duties and the customs duties on the import of foreign paper. By this time machinery had been extensively adopted in the paper industries of other countries and these industries were expanding rapidly, notably in the U.S.A., Germany and France. The resulting substantial increases in international production and trade in paper meant in turn extreme pressure on raw material supplies. Unsatisfactory and peculiarly inelastic supply conditions had for long been tending to make rags costly and many attempts to find substitutes had been made. Not until 1860 was any appreciable success achieved when the use of esparto grass for paper making was patented and put into commercial operation. Of far greater significance, however, were the numerous experiments in the use of wood pulp, carried on in this country and elsewhere, which culminated in the perfecting of the chemical processes of producing wood pulp in the 1880s. The modern paper industry is substantially based on wood pulp, and the advent of this as the major raw material meant a reorientation of the industry in many ways, although not causing any radical revisions in the machinery by which paper was actually made. It had substantial international repercussions in that it brought a new stimulus to the opening up of the great softwood forests of Scandinavia and Canada, in which countries integrated pulp and paper mills have been developed; at the same time the English industry became dependent for the bulk of its raw materials on imported substances. . . .

The industry's technical history thus has three landmarks: three crucial innovations—a medieval mechanization of the preparatory processes akin to the mechanization of fulling; mechanization of the making process during the classical industrial revolution; and the introduction of a new raw material. This last development has brought the industry into the ambit of what has been described as a 'second industrial revolution' (before the present tying of that label on to the expected consequences of the automatic factory), or, indeed, the fifth if we follow Schumpeter's numbering and terminology.

III

What light does this shed on the various industrial revolutions?

To take the first those for which there are relevant statistical series: those covering the period including the classical industrial revolution exhibit a highly characteristic pattern. Fig. 1 reveals just the picture of steeply rising output which we have come to associate with large numbers of individual industries, with population growth, overseas trade, imports of raw cotton and so forth, during this period of English economic history.[7]

It is, in short, a typical picture. The machine brought a great increase in productivity and did away with the great dependence on skilled paper-making labour. Mills became bigger, new and larger mills sprang up in Lancashire, near the coalfields and the new towns of the north; those in the remoter counties began to disappear. Increasing production was, as usual, matched by a declining total number of mills. The whole picture, in short, is one of the classical industrial revolution *in one industry*: the first of the uses to which, as suggested above, the term is sometimes put.

What of the 'second' or 'fifth' or 'twentieth century' industrial revolutions? How does paper fit into what Schumpeter called 'the Kondratieff of electricity, chemistry and motors'? Fig. 2 exhibits the same picture for this period as did Fig. 1 for the earlier period.[8]

Here, then, in purely quantitative terms there appears to be a repetition of the 'industrial revolution' process as applied to one industry. And, moreover, we know too that it was accompanied by the major reorientation of the industry already described, by the new dependence on imported raw materials as reflected in the parallel

---

[7] [Details of the sources from which these and the following graphs were constructed will be found in the Appendix published with the original article.]

[8] Imports of paper-making materials comprised rags, esparto and wood pulp.

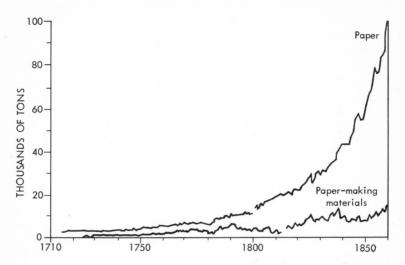

FIG. 1. English and U.K. paper production, 1714–1860, and imports of paper-making materials, 1727–1860.

movements of output and import curves, by changes in location and by increases in the size of mills. There was a continued and corresponding decline in numbers of mills in conjunction with steeply rising output; in the U.K. as a whole the number fell from rather over 400 in the 1850's to under 200 today, whilst during that century output had multiplied about 30 times. Behind the mere shape of these curves lies a complex pattern of changes in techniques, organization and industrial structure. Today the industry and its imported raw materials are of major importance in the country's economy. The increases in output during the 1920's and 1930's were in striking contrast to the depression which affected so many industries. At once a very old industry, it also apparently behaved like a typical 'new' industry.

How are we to assess these patterns of industrial growth? If the use of the term 'industrial revolution' in its application to a single industry is allowed, then it seems clearly evident that we must say that the paper industry has passed through two such revolutions. But are we justified in accepting the figures presented in this way, each shaped, so to speak, in the comparatively small mould of a hundred or a hundred and fifty years? These are the conventional dishes in which the 'revolutions' are so frequently cooked. But if we take the long-period view, which our figures allow, and at the same time plot these figures as growth curves, the picture appears in a rather different light.

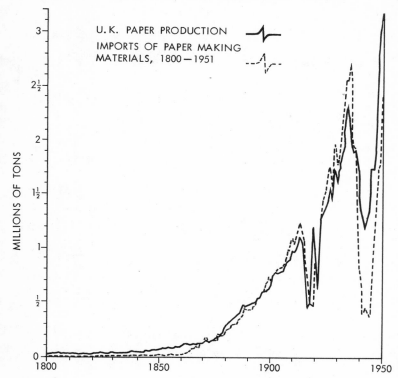

FIG. 2. U.K. paper production and imports of paper-making materials, 1800–1951.

From this it is equally clearly evident that the second 'industrial revolution' in the industry offers nothing more, in quantitative terms, than a continuation of the rate of growth initiated during the classical industrial revolution period. Even this does not show up very clearly but it appears to start with two changes from the comparative stagnation of the early decades of the eighteenth century: one commencing between 1740 and 1750 and another between 1800 and about 1810. The introduction of wood pulp is scarcely visible.

Much has been written about the shape of industrial growth curves.[9]

[9] As well as Schumpeter, *op. cit.*, see: S. Kuznets, *Secular Movements in Production and Prices* (New York, 1930); W. W. Rostow, *The Process of Economic Growth*, New York, 1952; R. Glenday, 'Long Period Economic Trends', in *Journal of the Royal Statistical Society*, CI, 1938; also W. Hoffman, 'The Growth of Industrial Production in Great Britain: a Quantitative Study', in *Econ. Hist. Rev.*, 2nd series, Vol. II, 1949–50, pp. 162–180.

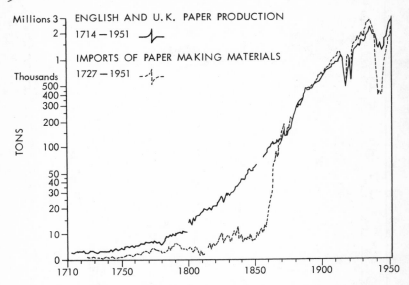

FIG. 3. English and U.K. paper production (1714–1951) and imports of paper-making materials, 1727–1951 (log. scale).

Professor Rostow has written: 'In general, although a phase of increasing rate of growth may occur in the very early stages of an industry, these growth patterns appear to follow roughly the course of a logistic curve; that is, they exhibit regular retardation'.[10] Warnings have been duly uttered to the effect that although 'we can see the curve of growth as logistic rather than exponential', this is not 'to suggest that all growth curves will be of this type'. . . .[11] In the case of the paper industry it is clearly evident that it was only the discovery of wood pulp which prevented the regular retardation from showing itself earlier.

It is very questionable whether such quantitative data can be used as 'pieces of economic history',[12] without at the same time considering in detail the technical developments which lie behind them. The continuation of the same growth rate in paper was entirely dependent on

[10] Rostow, *op. cit.*, p. 100.
[11] Hoffman, *loc. cit.*, p. 166.
[12] Especially in the manner followed by Hoffman both in the article cited above and in the uncritical acceptance of various statistics (including those for paper in the eighteenth century) which go to make up his index of Britain's industrial production. See his 'Ein Index der industriellen Produktion für Grossbritannien seit dem 18. Jahrhundert', in *Weltwirtschaftliches Archiv*, 1934 (II), p. 383.

the discovery of a *substitute,* in this case for raw material. If paper made from wood pulp were to be regarded as a different substance from that made from rags (which chemically it is *not,* . . .), then there would already be a logistic curve for rag paper followed by another, still as yet of the exponential type but likely to show retardation as soon as the softwood forests begin to be exhausted. The curve of the imports of paper-making materials in Fig. 3 gives some indication of this.[13] If figures existed for the production of papyrus, parchment and paper, one would *a priori* expect to see, for what might be called the 'Writing Materials Industry', a sort of family of successive logistic curves, the envelope of which would trace out a curve which would not yet show signs of permanent retardation in growth. Fig. 4 showing the output curves of hand-made paper and then its successor machine-made paper will serve as an illustration of this.

Two questions follow from this: how far can such an argument be generalized to apply to other industries, and—the old chestnut—what constitutes an industry? If we are willing to allow a certain common-sense elasticity in answering the latter, especially in the general direction of end uses to which products are put, it is not difficult to think of many examples which fit this pattern of industrial growth. The argument applies equally, for instance, to the development of the natural and then the synthetic fibre industry; at an earlier stage in the history of English and European textiles, the substitution of the 'New Draperies' for some of the older types of cloth offers a similar illustration. It applies also to the successive substitutions, first, of cheap iron (both cast and wrought), for wood, leather and other earlier constructional materials, and then after the 1860s, of steel for iron. The rise and fall of charcoal output, had we the figures, could be set against that of coal and the latter, in turn, matched with the statistics of the oil rush. The statistics of raw material imports and, in some instances, of exports in such industries as these would show appropriate changes comparable to those revealed above for the supply of paper-making materials.

Successive indices of this type reveal the constant change, the continual posing and solving of technical and economic problems in a manner in which national industrial growth curves, themselves composed of curves for conventional 'industries', do not. Indeed, the latter

---

[13] This has, of course, a national coverage only and consequently the shape of the curve is partly due to the fact that increasing world demand for wood pulp, together with the growth of integrated pulp and paper mills in the forest areas, have to some extent put the English industry in an economically disadvantageous position.

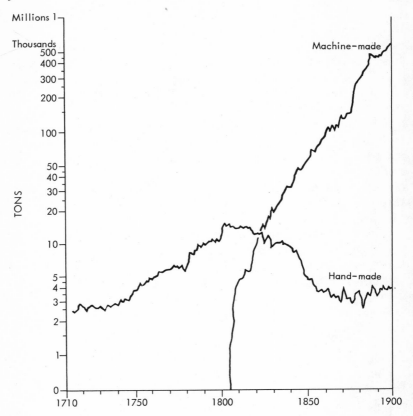

Fig. 4. English and U.K. production of hand-made and machine-made paper, 1714–1900 and 1806–1900 (log. scale).

often conceal more than they reveal. What is the steel industry or the metallurgical industry or the transport industry or the textile industry for the purposes of tracing the course of industrial growth? Schumpeter noted 'the broad fact of great steadiness in long-time increase . . . both in the sense of a rough constancy of the gradient of the trend and in the sense of what, merely by way of formulating a visual impression, we may term the general dominance or trend over fluctuations'. He illustrated this by reference to industrial production indices relating to Great Britain for 1785–1914 and U.S.A. and Germany from the 1860s to 1914. But in the truly long run, in the long focus of history, what exactly does this mean? Or again, what is the value to the economic historian of a production index in which even the classical industrial revolution can be made if not quite to disappear at least to appear as no more than a small change in the industrial growth rate? [14]

Now the studies, mostly by economists and statisticians, in which appear such quantitative analyses of industrial growth, have not paid over much attention to the question of how the concept of the industrial revolution, as otherwise used by historians, should appear in these series. But it seems clear that if we are to accept the arguments outlined above, the term 'industrial revolution', when referring to particular industries in their conventional forms, can be applied to every innovation which simply *maintains* the existing rate of growth of output.

If this appears to be a detraction from the significance of the term as normally understood and, indeed to be something of a *reductio ad absurdum,* then a remedy may perhaps lie in concentrating on *increase* in the growth rate, such as is registered in the paper industry, during the classical industrial revolution.[15] Should we, then, retain this crucial mechanization as indicative of the true 'industrial revolution in the paper industry'? Now if this is done, there seems to be no reason why we should not also accept earlier mechanization, however simple, which performed the same essential quantitative feat. And, moreover, if we examine that feat a little more closely it is seen to consist essentially of the mechanization or other crucial improvement of one process in the industry which, in turn, brings pressure to bear upon the other processes. If it could be shown to have thus operated, as is not unlikely, then the medieval application of water power to the rag-beating processes in the paper industry would seem to have a valid claim to the title. Doubtless, other industries might have similar pretensions: along with the stamping mill there may go the fulling mill, corn mill, the slitting mill, and the blast furnace with water-powered bellows, and more besides. Admittedly, figures are not available to prove that such innovations did in fact increase growth rates, but other sorts of evidence suggest that they certainly marked turning points in the development of the industries concerned and certainly had striking effects on industrial location. Professor Carus-Wilson is explicit about the nature of her 'industrial revolution' and the claims which she makes for it: 'the mechanizing of the first three cloth making processes during the eighteenth and nineteenth centuries is a commonplace of history, but the

[14] S. Kuznets, "Statistical Trends and Historical Changes", in *Econ. Hist. Rev.*, 2nd series, Vol. III, No. 3, 1951, p. 269: 'in the overall indices of production in Great Britain prepared by Walter Hoffman, the Industrial Revolution does not appear as a truly revolutionary upheaval'.

[15] Although if it were possible to extend the series further back in time, it is quite possible that this apparent increase would disappear.

mechanizing of the fourth during the thirteenth century, though it gave rise to an industrial revolution *no less remarkable* has attracted scarcely any attention'. (My italics.)

So now even if the late nineteenth and early twentieth century 'revolutions' are rejected, we are still left with two 'industrial revolutions' in the paper industry, and indeed on these arguments the same would apply to many other industries at many other times.

IV

Perhaps, then, the whole conception of an industrial revolution in a particular industry spells dangerous multiplicity. If safety does not lie this way, can it be found in the wider use of the term: in its application to industry as a whole or to the economy as a whole? Outside the classical industrial revolution, the example best known to economic historians is perhaps Professor Nef's English 'industrial revolution' of 1540–1640. In examining an era barren of detailed or continuous statistics, the assessment of its industrial development tends to be an admixture of various sorts of quantitative and non-quantitative evidence of one sort or another, the whole only too often amounting to a sample very far from random. Economic historians are indebted to Professor Nef for his fundamental researches into the coal industry, for pointing to industries once ignored and for unearthing the long roots of industrialization. But there is reason to suppose that the 'industrial revolution' which he has made his own owes more to the vigour and enthusiasm of his writing than to the typicality of his samples. The claims which he makes for his revolution have a familiar ring: 'The introduction of new industries and of new machinery, tools, and furnaces in the old industries, had brought about technical changes in the methods of mining and manufacturing *only less momentous* than those associated with the great inventions of the late eighteenth and early nineteenth centuries.' [16] (My italics.) In a more recent work this 'early English industrial revolution' is said to have marked 'the genesis of industrial civilization' and to have prepared the way for the eventual industrialization of the world.

Although it is not feasible here to embark upon a comprehensive examination of these claims, it is possible to give some indication of the way in which this 'revolution' has apparently been built up.

According to Professor Nef, 'tens of thousands of work people' were

---

[16] 'Progress of Technology', in *Econ. Hist. Rev.*, 1934, p. 22. Reprinted in *Essays in Economic History* ed. E. M. Carus-Wilson, 1954 reprinted 1962 as Vol. I. See also Nef, *Rise of the British Coal Industry*, I, p. 165.

swept into 'hundreds of new, capitalistically-owned enterprises', the introduction of which 'during the last sixty years of the sixteenth century opened an entirely fresh field for the growth of industrial capitalism'. Amongst such industries was paper making. For evidence on the scale of England's paper-making at this time, Professor Nef relies on what has been written about John Spilman's mill, at work at Dartford in 1588. That the paper mill of this period, with its water wheels, stampers, buildings, and apparatus, represented something much more substantial in the way of fixed capital than the weaver's cottage and loom is scarcely open to doubt. But that any appreciable number of mills were of the size which Spilman's was alleged to be is very unlikely for a century or more after 1588. Professor Nef has to admit that Thomas Churchyard in his poem about Spilman's mill 'probably exaggerated when he spoke of 600 workmen', confining him-self to the assertion that 'the enterprise certainly employed scores of hands'. But did it? And how many scores? And if it did, how many other paper mills were there that did? . . .

Did such 'capitalistically-owned enterprises' as these really help to open 'an entirely fresh field for the growth of industrial capitalism'? As with shipbuilding,[17] so with paper-making: Professor Nef's claims seem to owe much to untypical examples. It seems highly likely that a careful examination of other industries which figure in his revolution—mining, metal manufacture, alum and copperas making, and so on—would reveal this same method by which a national 'industrial revolu-tion' has been constructed out of a number of innovations in industry. This is not in the least to deny that the development of these industries marked a significant variation on domestic production or that they represented, taken together, an important phase in the slow growth of early industrialization; but this is quite different from inflating them into a 'industrial revolution' and equating this with the transformation wrought in the nineteenth century.

The main item, indeed, in many ways the basis, of Professor Nef's revolution is the coal industry. Here the evidence does not rest simply on increases in scale and capital outlay. The 'industrial revolution' he sees as ending with the Civil War; and thereafter 'although there was a recovery after 1660 and the production of British coal, cloth and paper grew during the eight decades that followed the Restoration of that year, it was not until at least the 1750s that the rate of increase

---

[17] See D. C. Coleman, 'Naval Dockyards under the Later Stuarts', in *Econ. Hist. Rev.*, Vol. IV, No. 2, December 1953, for this aspect of Professor Nef's revolution'.

in industrial output was again as rapid as during the period 1540–1640'. No adequate statistical series are available to support this statement; it rests upon the type of non-quantitative evidence mentioned above, together with Professor Nef's own estimates relating to the growth of the British coal industry; these show a 14-fold increase between 1551–60 and 1681–90, a 3-fold increase in the following century and a 23-fold increase between 1781–90 and 1901–10. Further, the fact that there appears to be a 14-fold increase in one century and only a 3-fold increase in the next is used, together with its repercussions and other allied changes, as part evidence for an industrial revolution in the economy as a whole.

There is one obvious objection to this: comparatively large rates of increase will naturally appear whilst absolute amounts are small and/or whilst an industry is new. This can be clearly seen in the growth of such modern industries as oil, aluminium, synthetic fibres and many others: it is reflected, as has been shown, in the early years of the growth of machine-made paper and in the import of paper-making materials into this country after the invention of wood pulp (see Figs. 3 and 4). The charcoal-coal relationship is, indeed, just such a thing as is illustrated in Fig. 4 and is consequently open to the same objections as a candidate for the title of 'industrial revolution', quite apart from its use as a basis for extending the revolution to the country as a whole.

In all this Professor Nef was supported by Schumpeter who, believing the term to be outmoded and misleading, held the classical industrial revolution to be 'on a par with at least two similar events which preceded it and at least two more which followed it'. To Schumpeter these revolutions were long cyclical movements of the sort detected by Kondratieff. He firmly rejected the idea that the industrial revolution was a 'unique event or series of events that created a new economic order'. Indeed, we can hear exactly the same sort of claims as those made by Professors Carus-Wilson and Nef: writing of the Kondratieff beginning in 1898, Schumpeter described it as being caused by an 'economic revolution *analogous in every respect* to the "industrial revolution" of text-book fame'. (My italics.)

.   .   .   .

VI

How, then, are we to accept these various revolutions? What relation do they bear to the classical industrial revolution? Are they all identical phenomena? Although the Kondratieffs of Schumpeter's ingenious cyclical model may seem to be identical phenomena within that structure, they are not historically identical in any sense other than that in which certain not very adequate quantitative series can make them seem so. Nor again are they the same as a thirteenth-century revolution in the process of fulling, although such a revolution could form a vital constituent of a Schumpeterian 'industrial revolution'.

Perhaps it is time for a new 'historical revision' of the 'industrial revolution'. When Mr. H. L. Beales wrote his historical revisions twenty-six years ago,[18] the dangers were not simply that it should be considered a unique phenomenon but that it was arbitrarily limited in time, without roots in the past and truncated in its development and application by the inadequacy of the word 'industrial' and the overtones of the word 'revolution'. Since then much has been done to show that the classical industrial revolution had its roots in the scientific thought and economic activity of the sixteenth and seventeenth centuries, and that it came to bear its fruit in decades long after the first Reform Bill was passed. But today the dangers are different: today we have too many industrial revolutions and too many ways of discovering them.

On its technical side *the* industrial revolution was the first major and large-scale success in man's efforts to apply his growing mastery of natural forces to economic production. It transformed this country in a way in which no country had ever before been transformed; and the process of industrialization which is still transforming once backward areas is the carrying abroad of this industrial revolution. Modern advances in science spring from the roots which first flowered so spectacularly in the seventeenth century, and modern advances in the interrelation of science and economic change (such as automatic controls) spring from that other first flowering which was the industrial revolution.

But, of course, it had aspects other than the technical. Professor Ashton has said of it that 'the changes were not merely "industrial" but also social and intellectual', and has justified his use of the term by noting that it 'has been used by a long line of historians and has become so firmly embedded in common speech that it would be pedantic to offer a substitute'.[19] And to keep it firmly embedded in common speech and give it a meaning which it deserves we should retain for it the significance which it was given by the earlier writers:

[18] H. L. Beales, 'Historical Revisions: The Industrial Revolution', in *History* n.s., **XIV** (1929), 125–29.

[19] T. S. Ashton, *The Industrial Revolution* (London, 1948), p. 2.

by Porter,[20] for instance, writing in economic and technical terms of changes radically affecting not simply industry but the country's whole economy, its social structure and its modes of thought and action. The term should not be applied to certain technical or economic innovations in particular industries which either maintain or increase the growth rate, nor can we deduce an industrial revolution simply from observing the existence in the appropriate figures of an increase in the growth rate of several industries. It is necessary to go beyond the curves of industrial growth and beyond mere mechanization to the vital conjuncture of changes in which population growth, large-scale and extensive industrial investment, and the remarkably pervasive effects of the application of science to industry are amongst the most important in producing the rapidly cumulative process of industrialization. This use of the term —the third of those mentioned earlier—as well as conforming to the classical English industrial revolution, would at the same time approximately conform to the process sometimes now called, as by Professor Rostow, the 'take-off' into industrialization. In this usage we avoid the danger of equating industrialization itself with industrial revolution, but reserve it for the initial and—in the long focus of history—comparatively sudden and violent change which launches the industrialized society into being, transforming that society in a way which none of the earlier so-called industrial revolutions ever did. At the same time we are retaining for the industrial revolution its uniqueness in the history of a country, but allowing its extension to others, as for instance in the conception of the Japanese industrial revolution, begun in the 1860s.

In this way, it should perhaps be possible to avoid depriving the term of its meaning, to avoid the path which at present seems to lead to the pointless notion of an economic history in which the absence of an 'industrial revolution' will soon be more significant than its presence. The qualitative changes wrought upon a society by the true industrial revolution would thus be emphasized. Though economic history may lean heavily on quantitative determinations, no amount of study of growth curves or the like will be adequate without searching examination of the technical, social, and economic problems which lie behind them.

. . . .

[20] G. R. Porter. *The Progress of the Nation* (London, 1851).

THE STRUCTURE OF ENTERPRISE IN THE NINETEENTH CENTURY *

The Cases of Britain and Germany

David S. Landes †

The Historical Experience

A. BRITAIN

The key problem is how Britain succeeded in effecting the Industrial Revolution without resort to the joint-stock company. (For the sake of brevity, I shall not discuss the peculiarities of Scottish business structure in this period.) In the mid-eighteenth century, on the eve of transformation, England had only a few corporations, most of them survivors from the pre-Bubble era, in fields like overseas trade (East India Co., Hudson's Bay Co.), banking (Bank of England), and insurance (London Assurance Corp.). There was also a larger number of unincorporated companies, operating mostly in these same areas, plus so-called cost-book mining ventures, the already customary 64-part ship groups, and turnpike and other trusts. A century later, Britain was the workshop of the world, with commercial and industrial units several times larger than those found elsewhere, larger by far than had once been thought feasible for a single man or small group. Yet the great majority of these enterprises, particularly in manufacturing industry, were proprietorships or ordinary partnerships. The joint-stock corporation was still essentially confined to the fields of 1750. In so far as it had widened its role, it had done so largely in what we would now call public utilities: canals and railroads, water works and gas supply, docks.

* Reprinted from the *Rapports* of the XIe Congrès International des Sciences Historiques, Vol. V: *Histoire Contemporaine* (Stockholm, 1960), pp. 107–28. Used by permission of Almqvist and Wicksell, Stockholm.

† David S. Landes is Professor of History at Harvard University. He is the author of *Bankers and Pashas: International Finance and Economic Imperialism in Egypt;* "Technological Change and Development in Western Europe, 1750–1914," *Cambridge Economic History*, Vol. VI; and articles on European economic and social history.

On the most superficial level, this neglect of what the French called the "principle of association" was due to legal impediments. By virtue of the Bubble Act of 1720, the creation of a joint-stock company with transferable shares and corporate status was possible only with the consent of the state; the usual enabling procedure came to be an act of Parliament. This consent was not easy to obtain and always costly. Manufacturing and trading enterprises, in particular, were rarely approved.

To be sure, promoters organized companies without permission, even in the face of prosecution. They made use of the device known as the deed of settlement to delegate control over the assets of the company to a small group of trustees, who behaved in fact like the board of a corporation. They even tried to achieve limitation of liability (notably in the case of insurance companies) by inscribing it in contracts with outside parties. We do not know as much about these "equitable companies" as we would like; in many cases we know of them only because they found their way into the courts. They were certainly much more numerous than the authorized corporations; and most of them continued to appear in the traditional fields of joint-stock activity. There were hardly any in manufacturing. The one exception, though closer in structure to the shipowning group, was the joint factories created by wool weavers in the West Riding in order to pool fulling, dyeing, and similar facilities.

This ingenious evasion of the law was effective so long as they prospered and did not get involved in litigation with outsiders. The Crown was inclined to leave them alone; in their internal disputes, they came under the jurisdiction of a tolerant Chancery, rather than the common law. Where others were concerned, however, they found it difficult to proceed at law and the courts held their liability to be unlimited. So that statute and usage did make a difference: the equitable company was necessarily of limited applicability.

Yet to explain the policy of more than a century by legal requirements is to misunderstand the role of law as an expression of the needs and values of a society. The question must simply be rephrased: why did Britain, in a period of unprecedented growth, not change the rules so as to facilitate the mobilization of capital and the creation of enterprise?

The positive reasons are more obvious. It was generally believed, with Adam Smith, that except in a few activities reducible to a routine or requiring resources beyond the means of an individual or small group, joint-stock companies would not be able to compete with private firms. Their establishment, therefore, would merely perturb business and lead to misallocation of resources. At the same time, unlimited liability was felt to be the foundation of commercial integrity; general incorporation was looked upon as subversive of morals, not to say unfair to those firms operating under more rigid standards. Ironically enough, there were some—those especially who feared new competition—who argued against the corporation on grounds both of inefficiency and differential advantage.

These objections of principle and interest were not really challenged until the third and fourth decades of the nineteenth century. The simple fact was that Britain did not need joint-stock companies to finance her industrial revolution. On the one hand, as the first in the field, she was able to build her plant from the ground up, as it were, beginning with rudimentary machines that were not too expensive for private purses and plowing profits into growth and technological advance. On the other, no country in the world was so responsive to economic opportunity. The society was open, to the point where Continental travelers of the eighteenth century speak of it as they were to speak later of the United States. Neither corporate privilege nor status barriers stood in the way of the movement of capital or persons. Moreover, the general respect accorded trade, especially by comparison with its denigration in other nations, encouraged persistence in enterprise. Indeed, agriculture itself was extensively commercialized, and the land-owning class was accustomed to rational employment of its fortunes, in mobile as well as "real" wealth. So that where the Continent saw a steady bleeding of business resources and talent by more honorific callings, and commercial success was usually the occasion for irrevocable retirement to landed gentility, in Britain the land returned what it received.

Similarly the structure of the firm was more open and rational than in the Continental countries. Everywhere the fundamental business unit was the individual proprietorship or partnership, but where, in a country like France, the partnership was almost always exclusively familial, British entrepreneurs were far more willing to enter into association with friends and friends of friends. This was especially true of heavy industry, where capital requirements were large even in the eighteenth century.

In sum, the initial requirements of industrialization were manageable within the traditional organizational framework. Subsequent growth, that is, from about 1800 on, was largely paid for by self-financing

and the transfer of savings from the nonindustrial to the manufacturing sector. In this regard, one cannot overestimate the importance of
a widely based system of financial institutions sensitive and responsive
to the needs of industry and trade. The basic unit was the local private
bank, familiar with the entrepreneurs and enterprise in its area and
ready to extend assistance that was nominally short-term (on the
security of bills of exchange) or callable on demand (overdraft) but
that in fact constituted indefinite revolving credit. Further, the banking
houses of the industrial North and Midlands were linked through the
bill brokers and discount houses of London to the rest of the country, so
that the surplus funds of the agricultural areas provided in effect much
of the working capital of industry.

This ability to grow without recourse to the joint-stock form was the
principal deterrent to the adoption of general incorporation in a
country generally quick to suit its laws to its needs. The one exception,
as noted above, was the field of public utilities, railroads in particular,
and there the legislature showed itself ready to grant the special charters
required. Over one hundred were authorized by 1844, and it would be
hard to exaggerate the contribution of these firms to the development of
the English capital market and the education of investors. The success
of railway securities made the acceptance of industrial securities in
general a matter of time. In the meanwhile, every period of cyclical
expansion saw promoters and investors press for more liberal arrangements for companies of any and all kinds. The demands found partial,
piecemeal satisfaction: in 1825 the centennial Bubble Act was repealed
and unincorporated joint-stock enterprises left to the ambiguous mercies
of the common law; the Trading Companies Bill of 1834 enabled the
Crown to grant by letters patent some of the privileges incident to
incorporation, in particular, the right to sue or be sued in the name of
an individual officer of the company; finally, the Act of 1844 required
unchartered joint-stock companies to register, gave them legal status,
and accorded them all the privileges of incorporation except limited
liability.

General limited liability did not come until 1856. Even then, banks
and insurance companies were excepted: the former were brought under
the new arrangements in 1858; the latter, by the general consolidation
Act of 1862. Interestingly enough, the first movers of the parliamentary
debates that led to the Act of 1856 were "middle class" philanthropists
desirous of facilitating the creation of co-operative working-men's associations. But the decisive push came from three sources: the promoters
who wanted to make the most of the euphoric economic expansion of

the fifties; the many investors who were looking for profitable placements in trade and industry now that "railroadization" was substantially
completed; and the triumph of liberal economic sentiment within and
without the business community, a triumph that washed away corn
laws, navigation acts, tariffs, and usury laws as well as restraints on
company formation.

Even so, victory was not easy; and this, in spite of developments
outside of Britain that seemed to demonstrate the potency and economic
desirability of joint-stock enterprise. In 1852 in Paris the Pereires
founded the Crédit Mobilier with the announced aim of mobilizing the
capital of small and medium savers for large-scale industrial undertakings. This was not the first joint-stock investment bank, but coming as
it did at a time of general prosperity to a business community awakened
by the disaster of 1848 to the dangers of securities flotation by firms of
unlimited liability, it precipitated an international revolution in the
organization of credit. Aside from the promotions of the Crédit Mobilier
itself and those of the older banks following in its wake as allies or
competitors, analogous finance companies sprang up throughout Europe
in the 1850's, especially in Germany, where, as the French Consul in
Leipzig noted, every little state insisted on its own banks of issue and
credit.

To all this ferment, England turned a disapproving back. She did
not need the joint-stock investment bank—for reasons noted above; and
the very ebullience of Continental finance gave her pause. Not until
automatic registration was possible were there serious efforts to found
comparable institutions in Britain. These were abortive, in part because
the commercial crisis of 1857–1859 temporarily precluded successful
promotions. Then in the 1860's, British entrepreneurs made up for lost
time by bringing out a swarm of finance companies—overt, and disguised as trading corporations, discount houses, etc. Unlike most of their
Continental counterparts, however, they did little for industry or transport, which did not need them, and concentrated instead in the more
lucrative field of short-term commercial loans. Many specialized in the
trade of exotic areas that had never known any credit but that of the
usurer; the risks were substantial, but the price of money fabulous. It
was a dangerous game that throve on the commodity speculation of the
period and came to an unhappy ending in the crash of 1866. From that
time, British banking eschewed speculative promotion and disguised
forms of long-term credit and returned to the classical tradition of short-
term paper and liquid assets. If anything, policy became more conservative than in the sanguine early decades of the century. An entrepreneur

of the late Victorian period might well have asked with the poet,
"Where are the overdrafts of yesteryear?"

In the meantime, the corporation as a form grew in importance—
without significant assistance from the banks. At first company formation followed the traditional pattern; the great majority of the new
corporate enterprises were in public utilities, banking, insurance, overseas trade. Only slowly did manufacturing industry make use of the new
form, and then, as might be expected, it was the capital-intensive
branches—shipbuilding, iron and steel, and new fields like electricity—
that took the lead. Cotton was a special case. On the one hand, capital
requirements were lower than in heavy industry; existing firms were
wealthy enough to respond to opportunity with previously accumulated
resources and traditional sources of credit; and no industry had been
more opposed to the liberalization of company law. Yet the cotton trade,
by its very size, had trained a multitude of would-be managers; the
moderate capital requirements were an encouragement to entry; and of
all textiles, none lent itself so well to routine management. The result
was such firms as the Oldham limiteds, some of which were built with
the one-pound notes of local shopkeepers, foremen, and even mill hands.

In so far as the public company invaded industry, it rested on local
financial support. London, though the acknowledged center of the
capital market, dealt primarily in funds, foreign and colonial securities,
and shares of the great national or imperial financial and commercial
institutions. Industrial stocks on the London exchange were confined
essentially to firms in the metropolitan area. Each of the provincial
centers in turn had its own board of local industrial enterprises: Manchester, its cotton firms; Birmingham, its hardware and arms manufactures; Newcastle, coal mines and the iron mills of the Cleveland basin.
As we have already noted in regard to banking, this local support for
enterprise was an old story in England. In some fields, as in the
financing of railway construction, it contrasted sharply with Continental
arrangements, and in general it reflected the remarkable accumulation
and dispersion of capital on the island.

The conditions of capital supply—the absence of powerful investment banks and the availability of local resources, within and without
the enterprise—go far to account for the persistence of traditional patterns of business organization and behavior into the twentieth century.
Whether these local resources were adequate compensation for the
absence of systematic industrial finance is a matter of debate. In any
event, Britain saw comparatively little of the financial-industrial giantism
that seemed the mark of a new economic order, what Sombart called

Hochkapitalismus. In so far as she did make use of the corporate form, she was interested more in the convenience and safety of limited liability than in the easy mobilization of capital for rapid expansion. On the eve of the World War, about four fifths of the 62,762 active joint-stock companies were private companies, that is, partnerships in a new guise. For these, and indeed for many of the so-called public companies, the corporate principle in no way altered the methods and spirit of management. The role of the family or of associations of friends remained decisive.

B. GERMANY

The contrast with Britain is striking. In 1815, on the eve of her industrial revolution, Germany was poor in capital and skills, both entrepreneurial and technical. The French invasions, for all the enlightenment they had brought, had cost Germany dear—like the wars of previous centuries. In spite of mergers and annexations, the land remained carved into a mosaic of sovereignties, whose ravel of boundaries combined with numerous, generally abusive tolls on rivers, bridges, and roads to hobble trade and limit accordingly industrial demand. Finally, allowing for regional differences, German society was far more closed than the British, presenting obstacles to the movement of labor and capital comparable to those offered to the shipment of goods. In short, the country was backward and materially and institutionally handicapped in its effort to catch up.

In the course of the next generation, many of these obstacles were removed: in particular, the reforms of Stein, gradually effected in Prussia and imitated in other states, freed the labor and capital markets from feudal-manorial restrictions, while the establishment of the Zollverein erased the political barriers to trade through a large part of the country. There remained, however, serious natural and material handicaps—not to be overcome until the coming of the railroad—as well as continued scarcity of capital and skills. German industry developed slowly after 1815—though faster after 1834—and not until the 1850's did it pick up the speed that was soon to be the wonder of Europe.

The acceleration of the fifties was directly related to changes in the structure of enterprise and the capital market. These came about, moreover, not through legal reforms, but entrepreneurial action, often in the face of hostile public opinion and unfavorable political arrangements.

Broadly speaking, German company law was very close to that of France. Under Napoleon, the Rhineland was governed by the French

Code de Commerce of 1807, with its tripartite classification of *sociétés en nom collectif, sociétés en commandite,* and *sociétés anonymes;* it retained this after annexation to Prussia. The rest of Prussia came under the Allgemeine Preussische Landrecht, a loose code that left considerable latitude for individual specifications in the case of joint-stock companies. The other states had their own laws—or absence of law. In practice, the tendency was to shift toward the arrangements of the Code de Commerce, which had one great virtue: a place and specifications for each of the business forms employed. In effect, it gave recognition to the joint-stock corporation as something acceptable and proposable, rather than something rare and extraordinary. All the same, the corporation remained a form apart: almost everywhere (Hamburg was a notable exception) the anonymous company with limited liability required the authorization of the state.

In practice then, the key question for the entrepreneur was the readiness of the state to grant authorization. The question was not posed very often before 1850. It took a decade for the first company based on the Code de Commerce to make its appearance; and in the period before 1843, Prussia—by far the most important of the German states in this regard—saw the formation of only 74 corporations (including railways), 40 of them under the regime of the Code. Their spheres of activity were just about the same as in Britain: with the exception of mining, which was beginning to outgrow the centuries-old *Gewerkschaft* form, no industry was much affected.[1]

The few attempts to found manufacturing corporations in Prussia found the government unsympathetic. In part its reasoning was negative: there was no clear need for corporate enterprise in industry (a

---

[1] The *Gewerkschaft* had the advantage in time of crisis of being able, at least in principle, to call on its members for additional contributions (*Zubüsse*); it was less suited than the corporation to rapid growth, however, partly because it was limited to its existing membership (until the Allgemeine Preussische Berggesetz of 1865, only 128 *Kuxe,* or shares, were permitted) or replacements thereof (rather than additions thereto), partly because its capital, unfixed and subject to change, was not always deemed suitable security for loans.

These limitations became serious in the 1830's, when the search for coal reached far beneath the marl cover of the northern Ruhr and initial costs of exploitation rose substantially. One side-effect was to create pressure for larger concessions, which in turn invited bigger outlays. Where the earlier *Gewerkschaften* were capitalized at thousands or tens of thousands of talers, a deep shaft in the 1830's usually cost at least 100,000 talers. Most of the new companies were capitalized at a half million or million talers. Fritz Schlüter, *Das Verhältnis von Gewerkschaft zur Aktiengesellschaft im Ruhrbergbau, die Verschiebungen und inneren Ursachen* (Kettwig-Ruhr, 1940), pp. 6–11; Agnes M. Prym, *Stäatswirtschaft und Privatunternehmung in der Geschichte des Ruhrkohlenbergbaus* (Essen, 1950), p. 24.

survival of the concept of the exceptional character of the corporation, requiring specific justification). More important, however, the Prussian bureaucracy was disturbed by the leverage that the joint-stock form gave to mobile as against landed wealth, and to certain business groups (bankers and projectors, many of them Jews) as against the more familiar class of "honest and dependable" small producers and merchants. The potential competition of private securities with government issues was another source of concern. Finally, all these fears were reinforced, especially during the railway boom of the forties, by moral considerations. The corporation became inextricably linked for many with stock jobbing—the word "agiotage" recurs repeatedly in the literature of the period; and with the triumph of Mammon—usually depicted with pseudo-Semitic features—over sobriety, industry, and all the other "German virtues". Hence the law of May 1844 forbidding trade in futures and trade of any kind in foreign securities; hence the persistent opposition of Prussia, Frankfurt, and other states to joint-stock investment banks. In general, the ideological and political hostility to the corporate principle was stronger in Germany than in Britain, if only because the potential effects of the new form were so much greater.

Yet this potential (one thinks of the physical analogy of the voltage of an electric current) assured its triumph. Already in the forties, the most clear-sighted and imaginative of the German businessmen and economists—in particular the Rhenish group; Mevissen, Camphausen, et al.—were asserting the need of special institutions to compensate for the poverty of the country and make possible investment on the scale required by modern industry. They did not use the jargon of economic development, but their position was identical with that of present-day economic historians who have spelled out the link between corporate enterprise and the investment bank on the one hand and backwardness on the other.[2]

The fervid plans of the forties had to mark time as a result of the revolution of 1848 and the consequent business crisis. The explosion of the 1850's was all the more powerful for the delay. These were years of prosperity throughout Europe, and for Germany especially, this was the era of Westphalia's coming-of-age (the first coke blast-furnace in the Ruhr was not blown in until the late forties) and of the triumph of the joint-stock investment bank.[3] Professor Cameron has described in some

---

[2] [See the article by A. Gerschenkron on "Economic Backwardness in Historical Perspective," reprinted in this volume.]

[3] The rapidity of the expansion may be judged from the statistics given by Leo Kluitmann in *Der gewerbliche Geld und Kapitalverkehr im Ruhrgebiet im 19. Jahrhundert* (Bonn, 1931), p. 44 [Reprinted in this volume, p. 108.]

JOINT-STOCK COMPANY FORMATION IN PRUSSIA

	Iron and Steel		Mineral Fuel		Total	
	Number	Capital (talers)	Number	Capital (talers)	Number	Capital (talers)
To 1800	1	120,000	—	—	1	120,000
1801–25	1	151,500	1	350,000	2	501,500
1826–50	2	2,166,667	9	11,620,000	11	13,786,667
1851–70	36	39,495,000	29	25,773,333	65	65,268,333

detail the role of French enterprise—in particular, that of the Pereires and the Crédit Mobilier—in introducing the finance company into Germany and the rest of the Continent.[4] Without seeking to depreciate this contribution, one may be permitted to situate it in its context. In the first place, German banking was, as already noted, already on the threshold of joint-stock industrial finance in the forties, partly under the influence of Saint-Simonian doctrine, partly owing to the Belgian example, partly by the very logic of circumstances. Secondly, German bank formation had an impetus and cadence all its own, far stronger and more rapid than the French. In this regard, political fragmentation was an advantage: what the German promoter could not get from Berlin, Frankfurt, or Karlsruhe, he could get from Darmstadt or Meiningen; whereas, owing to official hostility, the Crédit Mobilier did not see its first national rival until 1864. Finally, German investment banking was from the start different from the French, emphasizing its aversion to stock-market operations and its predilection for industrial development.

To be sure, much of this was talk, the kind of talk that Mevissen, for example, knew his stockholders wanted to hear. Yet it also reflected underlying economic divergences, in particular the difficulty encountered by French joint-stock banks in finding at home industrial ventures both desirous and deserving of their support, as against the abundance of financial opportunity in Germany. How much the real opportunities for development were in fact inferior in France—by reason of inadequate raw materials, for example—is not easy to say. I would contend, however, that the structure of enterprise did much to shape the relations between banks and industry, and that where the French private firm,

[4] Rondo Cameron, "The Crédit Mobilier and the Economic Development of Europe," *Journal of Political Economy*, LXI (1953), 461–88; "Some French Contributions to the Industrial Development of Germany, 1840–1870," *Journal of Economic History*, XVI (1956), 281–321; "Founding the Bank of Darmstadt," *Explorations in Entrepreneurial History*, VIII (1955–56), 113–30 (a translation of the last, with additional documents, appeared in *Tradition*, II [1957], 104–31).

with its closed familial character, tended to avoid outside financial assistance except *in extremis,* the German firm was more open, more ready to accept investments or loans from others. Moreover, there was a difference in timing. France in mid-century had an established industrial cadre, composed largely of family enterprises; conversion of these to new ways was difficult. Germany, more backward, had to create much of her industry *de novo;* and it was the bankers and other promoters who developed it in the form of joint-stock corporations.

In any event, the tie between industry and finance in Germany became ever closer, particularly in fields like mining, metallurgy, machine construction, chemicals, and electrical engineering, where capital requirements and cost of entry were high. It was not only that the banks floated the securities of new or expanding enterprises; the point is that they retained an interest in their offspring and exercised a continuing influence on, if not control over, their operations. Moreover, with increasing financial concentration, a few large banks—notably the four "D" Banks (Deutsche Bank, Dresdner Bank, Darmstädter Bank, Discontogesellschaft)—came to dominate entire industrial and commercial sectors. Nowhere else in western Europe, with the exception of Austria and its Creditanstalt, was there anything like it; small wonder that it was German scholars and polemicists who developed the concept of "finance capitalism".

The implications of this institutional marriage of banking and industry have been abundantly commented; we need simply review them here:

1. The emergence of big business as a political power. This has been and remains a matter of debate. Marxists, for example, would argue that the diplomatic and colonial policies of the Bismarckian Reich already reflected faithfully the interests of finance capitalism. Others, pointing to the power of the landed gentry before the First World War, would push the date forward to Weimar and the advent of Hitler. Still others would deny the existence of a definable, cohesive financial influence on politics and diplomacy. The subject requires more research; the answer will necessarily be nuanced; and there is little likelihood that historians as a group will ever agree on a given solution.

2. The effect on the structure of enterprise and the organization of the market. The great banks were a force for stabilization of prices and output through cartelization once the interests of their industrial clients could be reconciled and merged. The turning point came around 1890, when vertical integration had proceeded—thanks in large part to bank financing and promotion—to the point where there were few

major enterprises left specializing in only part of the process of manufacture and hence fearful of the effects of cartelization on the costs of
their raw and semiprocessed materials.

3. The contribution of finance capitalism to economic development.
The point is related to the preceding. In theory, cartelization should
give rise to a misallocation of resources and thereby retard growth; in
fact there is good reason to believe that the system generally used of
proportioning market shares to capacity pushed cartel members to invest
more and faster than they would have done otherwise. In the long run,
thanks in part to dumping in times of market contraction, these investments paid well. Whether they paid better than alternative placements
might have done is a question the historian cannot answer in any
meaningfully quantitative way. And it is even more difficult to estimate
the impact on overall growth of any deviation of investment from some
theoretical optimum.[5] Finally, given the importance of credit creation
in the process, there is no way of saying whether equivalent alternative
investment would necessarily have occurred in the absence of this
industrial expansion; very likely not.

If the direct macroeconomic effects of German finance capitalism
are problematical, it may still be argued that the system promoted the
rationalization of those branches of industry it embraced and thereby
made possible their successful competition with those of other countries.
Thus the late nineteenth century saw German production pass that of
Britain in a number of key fields, most notably iron and steel, while
her development of newer branches like chemicals or electricity was
the wonder of Europe and the world. Essentially this achievement was
the result of favorable resources and an institutional environment that
furnished excellent engineers and technicians and accorded them a
place of honor in industry. On the other hand, it is clear that the
opportunities for this talent would have been significantly limited in a
system of family enterprises, recruiting on a personal rather than an
impersonal basis. Moreover the great investment banks, with their
research departments and their direct interest in the promotion of
integrations, amalgamations, and other transactions susceptible of being
presented, hence sold, to the public as steps in the direction of greater
efficiency, contributed powerfully to this pursuit of optimum structure
and performance.

[5] [Modern econometric techniques, however, can yield a first approximation to
such costs—so long as the ramifications of the postulated change or deviation are
not pursued beyond first or second remove. For a pioneer example of this kind
of analysis, see Robert W. Fogel, *Railroads and American Economic Growth:
Essays in Econometric History* (Baltimore, 1964)].

I have discussed this "technological rationality" of Germa. elsewhere and contrasted it with the traditional "pecuniary r: of the economist.[6] The terminology is in one sense mislea "technological rationality" of the Germans brought greater pecuniary returns in the long run than the "pecuniary rationality" of, say, the British. *Ex post,* the only difference between the two systems would seem to be one of calculation: the German industrialist and financier had a longer time horizon and included in their estimates exogenous variables of continuing technological change that their British competitor held constant. *Ex ante,* however—that is, from the standpoint of the investment decision—there was a crucial difference in motivation that goes far to explain why German enterprise behaved the way it did. I would argue that the German entrepreneur often sought technological modernity for its own sake, that is, had made the means the end, and that thanks to a number of wider economic and historical considerations, he found he had chosen the profitable path. All of which is not intended to diminish the importance of these wider considerations, but rather to complete the picture by underlining the importance of the structure of enterprise for the total process of development.

[6] "Technological Change and Industrial Development," *Cambridge Economic History,* VI, 578–84.

ECONOMIC BACKWARDNESS IN HISTORICAL PERSPECTIVE *

Alexander Gerschenkron †

A historical approach to current problems calls perhaps for a word of explanation. Unlike so many of their predecessors, modern historians no longer announce to the world what inevitably will, or at least what

* Reprinted by permission of the publishers from Alexander Gerschenkron, *Economic Backwardness in Historical Perspective,* pp. 5–26. Cambridge, Mass.: The Belknap Press of Harvard University Press, Copyright 1962, by the President and Fellows of Harvard College.

† Alexander Gerschenkron is Walter S. Barker Professor of Economics in Harvard University. He is the author of numerous books and articles in European economic history, among them *Bread and Democracy in Germany* and *Economic Backwardness in Historical Perspective,* a collection of his essays.

ideally should, happen. We have grown modest. The prophetic fervor was bound to vanish together with the childlike faith in a perfectly comprehensible past whose flow was determined by some exceedingly simple and general historical law. Between Seneca's assertion of the absolute certainty of our knowledge of the past and Goethe's description of history as a book eternally kept under seven seals, between the *omnia certa sunt* of the one and the *ignorabimus* of the other, modern historical relativism moves gingerly. Modern historians realize full well that comprehension of the past—and that perforce means the past itself —changes perpetually with the historian's emphasis, interest, and point of view. The search is no longer for a determination of the course of human events as ubiquitous and invariant as that of the course of the planets. The iron necessity of historical processes has been discarded. But along with what John Stuart Mill once called "the slavery of antecedent circumstances" have been demolished the great bridges between the past and the future upon which the nineteenth-century mind used to travel so safely and so confidently.

Does this mean that history cannot contribute anything to the understanding of current problems? Historical research consists essentially in application to empirical material of various sets of empirically derived hypothetical generalizations and in testing the closeness of the resulting fit, in the hope that in this way certain uniformities, certain typical situations, and certain typical relationships among individual factors in these situations can be ascertained. None of these lends itself to easy extrapolations. All that can be achieved is an extraction from the vast storehouse of the past of sets of intelligent questions that may be addressed to current materials. The importance of this contribution should not be exaggerated. But it should not be underrated either. For the quality of our understanding of current problems depends largely on the broadness of our frame of reference. Insularity is a limitation on comprehension. But insularity in thinking is not peculiar to any special geographic area. Furthermore, it is not only a spatial but also a temporal problem. All decisions in the field of economic policies are essentially decisions with regard to combinations of a number of relevant factors. And the historian's contribution consists in pointing at *potentially* relevant factors and at *potentially* significant combinations among them which could not be easily perceived within a more limited sphere of experience. These are the questions. The answers themselves, however, are a different matter. No past experience, however rich, and no historical research, however thorough, can save the living generation the creative task of finding their own answers and shaping their own future. The following remarks, therefore, purport to do no more than to point at some relationships which existed in the past and the consideration of which in current discussions might prove useful.

The Elements of Backwardness

A good deal of our thinking about industrialization of backward countries is dominated—consciously or unconsciously—by the grand Marxian generalization according to which it is the history of advanced or established industrial countries which traces out the road of development for the more backward countries. "The industrially more developed country presents to the less developed country a picture of the latter's future." [1] There is little doubt that in some broad sense this generalization has validity. It is meaningful to say that Germany, between the middle and the end of the last century, followed the road which England began to tread at an earlier time. But one should beware of accepting such a generalization too wholeheartedly. For the half-truth that it contains is likely to conceal the existence of the other half—that is to say, in several very important respects the development of a backward country may, by the very virtue of its backwardness, tend to differ fundamentally from that of an advanced country.

It is the main proposition of this essay that in a number of important historical instances industrialization processes, when launched at length in a backward country, showed considerable differences, as compared with more advanced countries, not only with regard to the speed of the development (the rate of industrial growth) but also with regard to the productive and organizational structures of industry which emerged from those processes. Furthermore, these differences in the speed and character of industrial development were to a considerable extent the result of application of institutional instruments for which there was little or no counterpart in an established industrial country. In addition, the intellectual climate within which industrialization proceeded, its "spirit" or "ideology," differed considerably among advanced and backward countries. Finally, the extent to which these attributes of backwardness occurred in individual instances appears to have varied directly with the degree of backwardness and the natural industrial potentialities of the countries concerned.

Let us first describe in general terms a few basic elements in the industrialization processes of backward countries as synthesized from

[1] Karl Marx, *Das Kapital* (1st ed.), preface.

the available historical information on economic development of European countries [2] in the nineteenth century and up until the beginning of the First World War. Thereupon, on the basis of concrete examples, more will be said on the effects of what may be called "relative backwardness" upon the course of industrial development in individual countries.

The typical situation in a backward country prior to the initiation of considerable industrialization processes may be described as characterized by the tension between the actual state of economic activities in the country and the existing obstacles to industrial development, on the one hand, and the great promise inherent in such a development, on the other. The extent of opportunities that industrialization presents varied, of course, with the individual country's endowment of natural resources. Furthermore, no industrialization seemed possible, and hence no "tension" existed, as long as certain formidable institutional obstacles (such as the serfdom of the peasantry or the far-reaching absence of political unification) remained. Assuming an adequate endowment of usable resources, and assuming that the great blocks to industrialization had been removed, the opportunities inherent in industrialization may be said to vary directly with the backwardness of the country. Industrialization always seemed the more promising the greater the backlog of technological innovations which the backward country could take over from the more advanced country. Borrowed technology, so much and so rightly stressed by Veblen, was one of the primary factors assuring a high speed of development in a backward country entering the stage of industrialization. There always has been the inevitable tendency to deride the backward country because of its lack of originality. German mining engineers of the sixteenth century accused the English of being but slavish imitators of German methods, and the English fully reciprocated these charges in the fifties and sixties of the past century. In our own day, Soviet Russia has been said to have been altogether imitative in its industrial development, and the Russians have retorted by making extraordinary and extravagant claims. But all these superficialities tend to blur the basic fact that the contingency of large imports of foreign machinery and of foreign know-how, and the concomitant

[2] It would have been extremely desirable to transcend the European experience at least by including some references to the industrialization of Japan. Unfortunately, the writer's ignorance of Japanese economic history has effectively barred him from thus broadening the scope of his observations. The reader must be referred, however, to the excellent study by Henry Rosovsky, *Capital Formation in Japan, 1868–1940* (Glencoe, 1961), in which the validity of this writer's approach for Japanese industrial history is explicitly discussed.

opportunities for rapid industrialization with the passage of time, increasingly widened the gulf between economic potentialities and economic actualities in backward countries.

The industrialization prospects of an underdeveloped country are frequently judged, and judged adversely, in terms of cheapness of labor as against capital goods and of the resulting difficulty in substituting scarce capital for abundant labor. Sometimes, on the contrary, the cheapness of labor in a backward country is said to aid greatly in the processes of industrialization. The actual situation, however, is more complex than would appear on the basis of simple models. In reality, conditions will vary from industry to industry and from country to country. But the overriding fact to consider is that industrial labor, in the sense of a stable, reliable, and disciplined group that has cut the umbilical cord connecting it with the land and has become suitable for utilization in factories, is not abundant but extremely scarce in a backward country. Creation of an industrial labor force that really deserves its name is a most difficult and protracted process. The history of Russian industry provides some striking illustrations in this respect. Many a German industrial laborer of the nineteenth century had been raised in the strict discipline of a Junker estate which presumably made him more amenable to accept the rigors of factory rules. And yet the difficulties were great, and one may recall the admiring and envious glances which, toward the very end of the century, German writers like Schulze-Gaevernitz kept casting across the Channel at the English industrial worker, "the man of the future . . . born and educated for the machine . . . [who] does not find his equal in the past." In our time, reports from industries in India repeat in a still more exaggerated form the past predicaments of European industrializations in the field of labor supply.

Under these conditions the statement may be hazarded that, to the extent that industrialization took place, it was largely by application of the most modern and efficient techniques that backward countries could hope to achieve success, particularly if their industrialization proceeded in the face of competition from the advanced country. The advantages inherent in the use of technologically superior equipment were not counteracted but reinforced by its labor-saving effect. This seems to explain the tendency on the part of backward countries to concentrate at a relatively early point of their industrialization on promotion of those branches of industrial activities in which recent technological progress had been particularly rapid; while the more advanced countries, either from inertia or from unwillingness to require or impose sacrifices implicit in a large investment program, were more hesitant to carry out continual modernizations of their plant. Clearly, there are limits to such a policy, one of them being the inability of a backward country to extend it to lines of output where very special technological skills are required. Backward countries (although not the United States) were slow to assimilate production of modern machine tools. But a branch like iron and steel production does provide a good example of the tendency to introduce most modern innovations, and it is instructive to see, for example, how German blast furnaces so very soon become superior to the English ones, while in the early years of this century blast furnaces in still more backward southern Russia were in the process of outstripping in equipment their German counterparts. Conversely, in the nineteenth century, England's superiority in cotton textile output was challenged neither by Germany nor by any other country.

To a considerable extent (as in the case of blast furnaces just cited), utilization of modern techniques required, in nineteenth-century conditions, increases in the average size of plant. Stress on bigness in this sense can be found in the history of most countries on the European continent. But industrialization of backward countries in Europe reveals a tendency toward bigness in another sense. The use of the term "industrial revolution" has been exposed to a good many justifiable strictures. But, if industrial revolution is conceived as denoting no more than cases of sudden considerable increases in the rate of industrial growth, there is little doubt that in several important instances industrial development began in such a sudden, eruptive, that is, "revolutionary," way.

The discontinuity was not accidental. As likely as not the period of stagnation (in the "physiocratic" sense of a period of low rate of growth) can be terminated and industrialization processes begun only if the industrialization movement can proceed, as it were, along a broad front, starting simultaneously along many lines of economic activities. This is partly the result of the existence of complementarity and indivisibilities in economic processes. Railroads cannot be built unless coal mines are opened up at the same time; building half a railroad will not do if an inland center is to be connected with a port city. Fruits of industrial progress in certain lines are received as external economies by other branches of industry whose progress in turn accords benefits to the former. In viewing the economic history of Europe in the nineteenth century, the impression is very strong that only when industrial development could commence on a large scale did the tension between the preindustrialization conditions and the benefits expected from industrialization become sufficiently strong to overcome the existing obstacles and to liberate the forces that made for industrial progress.

This aspect of the development may be conceived in terms of Toynbee's relation between challenge and response. His general observation that very frequently small challenges do not produce any responses and that the volume of response begins to grow very rapidly (at least up to a point) as the volume of the challenge increases seems to be quite applicable here. The challenge, that is to say, the "tension," must be considerable before a response in terms of industrial development will materialize.

The foregoing sketch purported to list a number of basic factors which historically were peculiar to economic situations in backward countries and made for higher speed of growth and different productive structure of industries. The effect of these basic factors was, however, greatly reinforced by the use in backward countries of certain institutional instruments and the acceptance of specific industrialization ideologies. Some of these specific factors and their mode of operation on various levels of backwardness are discussed in the following sections.

The Banks

The history of the Second Empire in France provides rather striking illustrations of these processes. The advent of Napoleon III terminated a long period of relative economic stagnation which had begun with the restoration of the Bourbons and which in some sense and to some extent was the result of the industrial policies pursued by Napoleon I. Through a policy of reduction of tariff duties and elimination of import prohibitions, culminating in the Cobden-Chevalier treaty of 1860, the French government destroyed the hothouse in which French industry had been kept for decades and exposed it to the stimulating atmosphere of international competition. By abolishing monopoly profits in the stagnating coal and iron production, French industry at length received profitable access to basic industrial raw materials.

To a not inconsiderable extent, the industrial development of France under Napoleon III must be attributed to that determined effort to untie the strait jacket in which weak governments and strong vested interests had inclosed the French economy. But along with these essentially, though not exclusively, negative policies of the government,

French industry received a powerful positive impetus from a different quarter. The reference is to the development of industrial banking under Napoleon III.

The importance of that development has seldom been fully appreciated. Nor has it been properly understood as emanating from the specific conditions of a relatively backward economy. In particular, the story of the Crédit Mobilier of the brothers Pereire is often regarded as a dramatic but, on the whole, rather insignificant episode. All too often, as, for instance, in the powerful novels of Émile Zola, the actual significance of the developments is almost completely submerged in the description of speculative fever, corruption, and immorality which accompanied them. It seems to be much better in accord with the facts to speak of a truly momentous role of investment banking of the period for the economic history of France and of large portions of the Continent.

In saying that, one has in mind, of course, the immediate effects of creating financial organizations designed to build thousands of miles of railroads, drill mines, erect factories, pierce canals, construct ports, and modernize cities. The ventures of the Pereires and of a few others did all that in France and beyond the boundaries of France over vast areas stretching from Spain to Russia. This tremendous change in economic scenery took place only a few years after a great statesman and a great historian of the July monarchy assured the country that there was no need to reduce the duties on iron because the sheltered French iron production was quite able to cope with the iron needs of the railroads on the basis of his estimate of a prospective annual increase in construction by some fifteen to twenty miles.

But no less important than the actual economic accomplishments of a few men of great entrepreneurial vigor was their effect on their environment. The Crédit Mobilier was from the beginning engaged in a most violent conflict with the representatives of "old wealth" in French banking, most notably with the Rothschilds. It was this conflict that had sapped the force of the institution and was primarily responsible for its eventual collapse in 1867. But what is so seldom realized is that in the course of this conflict the "new wealth" succeeded in forcing the old wealth to adopt the policies of its opponents. The limitation of old wealth in banking policies to flotations of government loans and foreign-exchange transactions could not be maintained in the face of the new competition. When the Rothschilds prevented the Pereires from establishing the Austrian Credit-Anstalt, they succeeded only because they became willing to establish the bank themselves and to conduct it not as an old-fashioned banking enterprise but as a crédit mobilier, that is, as a bank devoted to railroadization and industrialization of the country.

This conversion of the old wealth to the creed of the new wealth points out the direction of the most far-reaching effects of the Crédit Mobilier. Occasional ventures of that sort had been in existence in Belgium, Germany, and France herself. But it was the great eruptive effect of the Pereires that profoundly influenced the history of Continental banking in Europe from the second half of the past century onward. The number of banks in various countries shaped upon the image of the Pereire bank was considerable. But more important than their slavish imitations was the creative adaptation of the basic idea of the Pereires and its incorporation in the new type of bank, the universal bank, which in Germany, along with most other countries on the Continent, became the dominant form of banking. The difference between banks of the crédit-mobilier type and commercial banks in the advanced industrial country of the time (England) was absolute. Between the English bank essentially designed to serve as a source of short-term capital and a bank designed to finance the long-run investment needs of the economy there was a complete gulf. The German banks, which may be taken as a paragon of the type of the universal bank, successfully combined the basic idea of the crédit mobilier with the short-term activities of commercial banks.

They were as a result infinitely sounder financial institutions than the Crédit Mobilier, with its enormously swollen industrial portfolio, which greatly exceeded its capital, and its dependence on favorable developments on the stock exchange for continuation of its activities. But the German banks, and with them the Austrian and Italian banks, established the closest possible relations with industrial enterprises. A German bank, as the saying went, accompanied an industrial enterprise from the cradle to the grave, from establishment to liquidation throughout all the vicissitudes of its existence. Through the device of formally short-term but in reality long-term current account credits and through development of the institution of the supervisory boards to the position of most powerful organs within corporate organizations, the banks acquired a formidable degree of ascendancy over industrial enterprises, which extended far beyond the sphere of financial control into that of entrepreneurial and managerial decisions.

It cannot be the purpose of this presentation to go into the details of this development. All that is necessary is to relate its origins and effects to the subject under discussion. The industrialization of England had proceeded without any substantial utilization of banking for long-term investment purposes. The more gradual character of the industrialization process and the more considerable accumulation of capital, first from earnings in trade and modernized agriculture and later from industry itself, obviated the pressure for developing any special institutional devices for provision of long-term capital to industry. By contrast, in a relatively backward country capital is scarce and diffused, the distrust of industrial activities is considerable, and, finally, there is greater pressure for bigness because of the scope of the industrialization movement, the larger average size of plant, and the concentration of industrialization processes on branches of relatively high ratios of capital to output. To these should be added the scarcity of entrepreneurial talent in the backward country.

It is the pressure of these circumstances which essentially gave rise to the divergent development in banking over large portions of the Continent as against England. The continental practices in the field of industrial investment banking must be conceived as specific instruments of industrialization in a backward country. It is here essentially that lies the historical and geographic locus of theories of economic development that assign a central role to processes of forced saving by the money-creating activities of banks. As will be shown presently, however, use of such instruments must be regarded as specific, not to backward countries in general, but rather to countries whose backwardness does not exceed certain limits. And even within the latter for a rather long time it was mere collection and distribution of available funds in which the banks were primarily engaged. This circumstance, of course, did not detract from the paramount importance of such activities on the part of the banks during the earlier industrialization periods with their desperate shortages of capital for industrial ventures.

The effects of these policies were far-reaching. All the basic tendencies inherent in industrial development in backward countries were greatly emphasized and magnified by deliberate attitudes on the part of the banks. From the outset of this evolution the banks were primarily attracted to certain lines of production to the neglect, if not virtual exclusion, of others. To consider Germany until the outbreak of World War I, it was essentially coal mining, iron- and steelmaking, electrical and general engineering, and heavy chemical output which became the primary sphere of activities of German banks. The textile industry, the leather industry, and the foodstuff-producing industries remained on the fringes of the banks' interest. To use modern terminology, it was heavy rather than light industry to which the attention was devoted.

Furthermore, the effects were not confined to the productive structure of industry. They extended to its organizational structure. The last three decades of the nineteenth century were marked by a rapid concentration movement in banking. This process indeed went on in very much the same way on the other side of the English Channel. But in Britain, because of the different nature of relations between banks and industry, the process was not paralleled by a similar development in industry.

It was different in Germany. The momentum shown by the cartelization movement of Germany industry cannot be fully explained, except as the natural result of the amalgamation of German banks. It was the mergers in the field of banking that kept placing banks in the positions of controlling competing enterprises. The banks refused to tolerate fratricidal struggles among their children. From the vantage point of centralized control, they were at all times quick to perceive profitable opportunities of cartelization and amalgamation of industrial enterprises. In the process, the average size of plant kept growing, and at the same time the interests of the banks and their assistance were even more than before devoted to those branches of industry where cartelization opportunities were rife.

Germany thus had derived full advantages from being a relatively late arrival in the field of industrial development, that is to say, from having been preceded by England. But, as a result, German industrial economy, because of specific methods used in the catching-up process, developed along lines not insignificantly different from those in England.

The State

The German experience can be generalized. Similar developments took place in Austria, or rather in the western sections of the Austrian-Hungarian Empire, in Italy, in Switzerland, in France, in Belgium, and in other countries, even though there were differences among the individual countries. But it certainly cannot be generalized for the European continent as a whole, and this for two reasons: (1) because of the existence of certain backward countries where no comparable features of industrial development can be discovered and (2) because of the existence of countries where the basic elements of backwardness appear in such an accentuated form as to lead to the use of essentially different institutional instruments of industrialization.

Little need be said with reference to the first type of country. The industrial development of Denmark may serve as an appropriate illustration. Surely, that country was still very backward as the nineteenth century entered upon its second half. Yet no comparable sudden spurts of industrialization and no peculiar emphasis on heavy industries could be observed. The reasons must be sought, on the one hand, in the paucity of the country's natural resources and, on the other hand, in the great opportunities for agricultural improvement that were inherent in the proximity of the English market. The peculiar response did not materialize because of the absence of the challenge.

Russia may be considered as the clearest instance of the second type of country. The characteristic feature of economic conditions in Russia was not only that the great spurt of modern industrialization came in the middle of the 1880s, that is to say, more than three decades after the beginning of rapid industrialization in Germany; even more important was the fact that at the starting point the level of economic development in Russia had been incomparably lower than that of countries such as Germany and Austria.

The main reason for the abysmal economic backwardness of Russia was the preservation of serfdom until the emancipation of 1861. In a certain sense, this very fact may be attributed to the play of a curious mechanism of economic backwardness, and a few words of explanation may be in order. In the course of its process of territorial expansion, which over a few centuries transferred the small duchy of Moscow into the huge land mass of modern Russia, the country became increasingly involved in military conflicts with the West. This involvement revealed a curious internal conflict between the tasks of the Russian government that were "modern" in the contemporaneous sense of the word and the hopelessly backward economy of the country on which the military policies had to be based. As a result, the economic development in Russia at several important junctures assumed the form of a peculiar series of sequences: (1) Basic was the fact that the state, moved by its military interest, assumed the role of the primary agent propelling the economic progress in the country. (2) The fact that economic development thus became a function of military exigencies imparted a peculiarly jerky character to the course of that development; it proceeded fast whenever military necessities were pressing and subsided as the military pressures relaxed. (3) This mode of economic progress by fits and starts implied that, whenever a considerable upsurge of economic activities was required, a very formidable burden was placed on the shoulders of the generations whose lifespan happened to coincide with the period of intensified development. (4) In order to exact effectively the great sacrifices it required, the government had to subject the reluctant population to a number of severe measures of oppression lest the burdens imposed be evaded by escape to the frontier regions in the southeast and east. (5) Precisely because of the magnitude of the governmental exactions, a period of rapid development was very likely to give way to prolonged stagnation, because the great effort had been pushed beyond the limits of physical endurance of the population and long periods of economic stagnation were the inevitable consequences. The sequences just mentioned present in a schematic way a pattern of Russian economic development in past centuries which fits best the period of the reforms under Peter the Great, but its applicability is by no means confined to that period.

What must strike the observer of this development is its curiously paradoxical course. While trying, as Russia did under Peter the Great, to adopt Western techniques, to raise output and the skills of the population to levels more closely approaching those of the West, Russia by virtue of this very effort was in some other respects thrown further away from the West. Broadly speaking, placing the trammels of serfdom upon the Russian peasantry must be understood as the obverse side of the processes of Westernization. Peter the Great did not institute serfdom in Russia, but perhaps more than anyone else he did succeed in making it effective. When in subsequent periods, partly because of point 2 and partly because of point 5 above, the state withdrew from active promotion of economic development and the nobility emancipated itself from its service obligations to the government, peasant serfdom was divested of its connection with economic development. What once was an indirect obligation to the state became a pure obligation toward the nobility and as such became by far the most important retarding factor in Russia's economic development.

Readers of Toynbee's may wish to regard this process, ending as it did with the emancipation of the peasantry, as an expression of the "withdrawal and return" sequence. Alternatively they may justifiably prefer to place it under the heading of "arrested civilizations." At any rate, the challenge-response mechanism is certainly useful in thinking about sequences of that nature. It should be noted, however, that the problem is not simply one of quantitative relationship between the volume of the challenge and that of the response. The crucial point is that the magnitude of the challenge changes the *quality* of the response and, by so doing, not only injects powerful retarding factors into the economic process but also more likely leads to a number of undesirable noneconomic consequences. To this aspect, which is most relevant to the current problem of industrialization of backward countries, we shall advert again in the concluding remarks of this essay.

To return to Russian industrialization in the eighties and the nineties of the past century, it may be said that in one sense it can be viewed as a recurrence of a previous pattern of economic development in the country. The role of the state distinguishes rather clearly the type of Russian industrialization from its German or Austrian counterpart.

Emancipation of the peasants, despite its manifold deficiencies, was an absolute prerequisite for industrialization. As such it was a negative action of the state designed to remove obstacles that had been earlier created by the state itself and in this sense was fully comparable to acts such as the agrarian reforms in Germany or the policies of Napoleon III which have been mentioned earlier. Similarly, the great judicial and administrative reforms of the sixties were in the nature of creating a suitable framework for industrial development rather than promoting it directly.

The main point of interest here is that, unlike the case of Western Europe, actions of this sort did not per se lead to an upsurge of individual activities in the country; and for almost a quarter of a century after the emancipation the rate of industrial growth remained relatively low. The great industrial upswing came when, from the middle of the eighties on, the railroad building of the state assumed unprecedented proportions and became the main lever of a rapid industrialization policy. Through multifarious devices such as preferential orders to domestic producers of railroad materials, high prices, subsidies, credits, and profit guaranties to new industrial enterprises, the government succeeded in maintaining a high and, in fact, increasing rate of growth until the end of the century. Concomitantly, the Russian taxation system was reorganized, and the financing of industrialization policies was thus provided for, while the stabilization of the ruble and the introduction of the gold standard assured foreign participation in the development of Russian industry.

The basic elements of a backward economy were, on the whole, the same in Russia of the nineties and in Germany of the fifties. But quantitatively the differences were formidable. The scarcity of capital in Russia was such that no banking system could conceivably succeed in attracting sufficient funds to finance a large-scale industrialization; the standards of honesty in business were so disastrously low, the general distrust of the public so great, that no bank could have hoped to attract even such small capital funds as were available, and no bank could have successfully engaged in long-term credit policies in an economy where fraudulent bankruptcy had been almost elevated to the rank of a general business practice. Supply of capital for the needs of industrialization required the compulsory machinery of the government, which, through its taxation policies, succeeded in directing incomes from consumption to investment. There is no doubt that the government as an *agens movens* of industrialization discharged its role in a far less than perfectly efficient manner. Incompetence and corruption of bureaucracy were great. The amount of waste that accompanied the process was formidable. But, when all is said and done, the great success of the policies pursued under Vyshnegradski and Witte is undeniable. Not only in their origins but also in their effects, the policies pursued by the Russian government in the nineties resembled closely those of the banks in Central Europe. The Russian state did not evince any interest in "light industry." Its whole attention was centered on output of basic industrial materials and on machinery production; like the banks in Germany, the Russian bureaucracy was primarily interested in large-scale enterprises and in amalgamations and coordinated policies among the industrial enterprises which it favored or had helped to create. Clearly, a good deal of the government's interest in industrialization was predicated upon its military policies. But these policies only reinforced and accentuated the basic tendencies of industrialization in conditions of economic backwardness.

Perhaps nothing serves to emphasize more these basic uniformities in the situation and the dependence of actual institutional instruments used on the degree of backwardness of the country than a comparison of policies pursued within the two halves of the Austrian-Hungarian monarchy, that is to say, within one and the same political body. The Austrian part of the monarchy was backward in relation to, say, Germany, but it was at all times much more advanced than its Hungarian counterpart. Accordingly, in Austria proper the banks could successfully devote themselves to the promotion of industrial activities. But across the Leitha Mountains, in Hungary, the activities of the banks proved altogether inadequate, and around the turn of the century the Hungarian government embarked upon vigorous policies of industrialization. Originally, the government showed a considerable interest in developing the textile industry of the region. And it is instructive to watch how, under the pressure of what the French like to call the "logic of things," the basic uniformities asserted themselves and how the generous government subsidies were more and more deflected from textile industries to promotion of heavy industries.

The Gradations of Backwardness

To return to the basic German-Russian paradigm: what has been said in the foregoing does not exhaust the pattern of parallels. The question remains as to the effects of successful industrializations, that is to say, of the gradual diminution of backwardness.

At the turn of the century, if not somewhat earlier, changes became apparent in the relationship between German banks and German industry. As the former industrial infants had grown to strong manhood, the original undisputed ascendancy of the banks over industrial enterprises could no longer be maintained. This process of liberation of industry from the decades of tutelage expressed itself in a variety of ways. Increasingly, industrial enterprises transformed connection with a single bank into cooperation with several banks. As the former industrial protectorates became economically sovereign, they embarked upon the policy of changing alliances with regard to the banks. Many an industrial giant, such as the electrical engineering industry, which could not have developed without the aid and entrepreneurial daring of the banks, began to establish its own banks. The conditions of capital scarcity to which the German banks owed their historical position were no longer present. Germany had become a developed industrial country. But the specific features engendered by a process of industrialization in conditions of backwardness were to remain, and so was the close relation between banks and industry, even though the master-servant relation gave way to cooperation among equals and sometimes was even reversed.

In Russia the magnificent period of industrial development of the nineties was cut short by the 1900 depression and the following years of war and civil strife. But, when Russia emerged from the revolutionary years 1905–1906 and again achieved a high rate of industrial growth in the years 1907–1914, the character of the industrialization processes had changed greatly. Railroad construction by the government continued but on a much smaller scale both absolutely and even more so relatively to the increased industrial output. Certain increases in military expenditures that took place could not begin to compensate for the reduced significance of railroad-building. The conclusion is inescapable that, in that last period of industrialization under a prerevolutionary government, the significance of the state was very greatly reduced.

At the same time, the traditional pattern of Russian economic development happily failed to work itself out. The retrenchment of government activities led not to stagnation but to a continuation of industrial growth. Russian industry had reached a stage where it could throw away the crutches of government support and begin to walk independently—and, yet, very much less independently than industry in contemporaneous Germany, for at least to some extent the role of the retreating government was taken over by the banks.

A great transformation had taken place with regard to the banks during the fifty years that had elapsed since the emancipation. Commercial banks had been founded. Since it was the government that had fulfilled the function of industrial banks, the Russian banks, precisely because of the backwardness of the country, were organized as "deposit banks," thus resembling very much the type of banking in England. But, as industrial development proceeded apace and as capital accumulation increased, the standards of business behavior were growingly Westernized. The paralyzing atmosphere of distrust began to vanish, and the foundation was laid for the emergence of a different type of bank. Gradually, the Moscow deposit banks were overshadowed by the development of the St. Petersburg banks that were conducted upon principles that were characteristic not of English but of German banking. In short, after the economic backwardness of Russia had been reduced by state-sponsored industrialization processes, use of a different instrument of industrialization, suitable to the new "stage of backwardness," became applicable.

Ideologies of Delayed Industrializations

Before drawing some general conclusions, a last differential aspect of industrialization in circumstances of economic backwardness should be mentioned. So far, important differences with regard to the character of industrial developments and its institutional vehicles were related to conditions and degrees of backwardness. A few words remain to be said on the ideological climate within which such industrialization proceeded.

Again we may revert to the instructive story of French industrialization under Napoleon III. A large proportion of the men who reached positions of economic and financial influence upon Napoleon's advent to power were not isolated individuals. They belonged to a rather well-defined group. They were not Bonapartists but Saint-Simonian socialists. The fact that a man like Isaac Pereire, who contributed so much, perhaps more than any other single person, to the spread of the modern capitalist system in France should have been—and should have remained to the end of his days—an ardent admirer of Saint-Simonian doctrines is on the face of it surprising. It becomes much less so if a few pertinent relationships are considered.

It could be argued that Saint-Simon was in reality far removed from being a socialist; that in his vision of an industrial society he hardly distinguished between laborers and employers; and that he considered the appropriate political form for his society of the future some kind of corporate state in which the "leaders of industry" would exercise major political functions. Yet arguments of that sort would hardly explain much. Saint-Simon had a profound interest in what he used to call the "most numerous and most suffering classes"; more importantly, Saint-Simonian doctrines, as expanded and redefined by the followers of the master (particularly by Bazard), incorporated into the system a good many socialist ideas, including abolition of inheritance and establishment of a system of planned economy designed to direct and to develop the economy of the country. And it was this interpretation of the doctrines which the Pereires accepted.

It is more relevant to point to the stress laid by Saint-Simon and his followers upon industrialization and the great task they had assigned to banks as an instrument of organization and development of the economy. This, no doubt, greatly appealed to the creators of the Crédit Mobilier, who liked to think of their institution as of a "bank to a higher power" and of themselves as "missionaries" rather than bankers. That Saint-Simon's stress upon the role to be played by the banks in economic development revealed a truly amazing—and altogether "un-utopian"—insight into the problems of that development is as true as the fact that Saint-Simonian ideas most decisively influenced the course of economic events inside and outside France. But the question remains: why was the socialist garment draped around an essentially capitalist idea? And why was it the socialist form that was so readily accepted by the greatest capitalist entrepreneurs France ever possessed?

It would seem that the answer must again be given in terms of basic conditions of backwardness. Saint-Simon, the friend of J. B. Say, was never averse to ideas of laissez-faire policies. Chevalier, the co-author of the Franco-English treaty of commerce of 1860 that ushered in the great period of European free trade, had been an ardent Saint-Simonian. And yet under French conditions a laissez-faire ideology was altogether inadequate as a spiritual vehicle of an industrialization program.

To break through the barriers of stagnation in a backward country, to ignite the imaginations of men, and to place their energies in the service of economic development, a stronger medicine is needed than

the promise of better allocation of resources or even of the lower price
of bread. Under such conditions even the businessman, even the
classical daring and innovating entrepreneur, needs a more powerful
stimulus than the prospect of high profits. What is needed to remove
the mountains of routine and prejudice is faith—faith, in the words of
Saint-Simon, that the golden age lies not behind but ahead of mankind.
It was not for nothing that Saint-Simon devoted his last years to the
formulation of a new creed, the New Christianity, and suffered Auguste
Comte to break with him over this "betrayal of true science." What
sufficed in England did not suffice in France.

Shortly before his death, Saint-Simon urged Rouget de Lisle, the
aged author of the "Marseillaise," to compose a new anthem, an
"Industrial Marseillaise." Rouget de Lisle complied. In the new hymn
the man who once had called upon "enfants de la patrie" to wage
ruthless war upon the tyrants and their mercenary cohorts addresses
himself to "enfants de l'industrie"—the "true nobles"—who would assure
the "happiness of all" by spreading industrial arts and by submitting the
world to the peaceful "laws of industry."

Ricardo is not known to have inspired anyone to change "God
Save the King" into "God Save Industry." No one would want to
detract from the force of John Bright's passionate eloquence, but in
an advanced country rational arguments in favor of industrialization
policies need not be supplemented by a quasi-religious fervor. Buckle
was not far wrong when in a famous passage of his *History* he presented the conversion of public opinion in England to free trade as
achieved by the force of incontrovertible logic. In a backward country
the great and sudden industrialization effort calls for a New Deal in
emotions. Those carrying out the great transformation as well as those
on whom it imposes burdens must feel, in the words of Matthew
Arnold, that

> . . . Clearing a stage
> Scattering the past about
> Comes the new age.

Capitalist industrialization under the auspices of socialist ideologies
may be, after all, less surprising a phenomenon than would appear at
first sight.

Similarly, Friedrich List's industrialization theories may be largely
conceived as an attempt, by a man whose personal ties to Saint-Si-
monians had been very strong, to translate the inspirational message
of Saint-Simonism into a language that would be accepted in the

.nan environment, where the lack of both a preceding political
olution and an early national unification rendered nationalist senti-
.ent a much more suitable ideology of industrialization.

After what has been just said it will perhaps not seem astonishing
that, in the Russian industrialization of the 1890s, orthodox Marxism
can be said to have performed a very similar function. Nothing reconciled the Russian intelligentsia more to the advent of capitalism in
the country and to the destruction of its old faith in the mir and the
artel than a system of ideas which presented the capitalist industrialization of the country as the result of an iron law of historical development. It is this connection which largely explains the power wielded
by Marxist thought in Russia when it extended to men like Struve and
in some sense even Milyukov, whose Weltanschauung was altogether
alien to the ideas of Marxian socialism. In conditions of Russian "absolute" backwardness, again, a much more powerful ideology was
required to grease the intellectual and emotional wheels of industrialization than either in France or in Germany. The institutional gradations
of backwardness seem to find their counterpart in men's thinking about
backwardness and the way in which it can be abolished.

THE "GREAT DEPRESSION" *

Maurice Dobb †

What has become known as the Great Depression, which started
in 1873 and, broken by bursts of recovery in 1880 and 1888, continued
into the middle '90's, has come to be regarded as forming a watershed
between two stages of Capitalism: the earlier vigorous, prosperous and
flushed with adventurous optimism; the later more troubled, more
hesitant and, some would say, already bearing the marks of senility

* Reprinted from *Studies in the Development of Capitalism* by Maurice Dobb,
pp. 300–19. Revised edition 1963. Used by permission of International Publishers
Co., Inc. (New York) and Routledge & Kegan Paul, Ltd. (London).

† Maurice Dobb is Fellow of Trinity College and Reader in Economics in
Cambridge University. He is the author of books and articles in labor economics,
the Soviet economy, and economic growth. Among his publications are *Capitalist
Enterprise and Social Progress, Wages, Soviet Planning and Labour in Peace and
War*, and *An Essay on Economic Growth and Planning*.

and decay. This was the period of which Engels spoke his well-known phrase about "the breakdown of . . . England's industrial monopoly", in which the English working class would "lose its privileged position" and "there (would) be Socialism again in England".[1] About its character and significance as well as its causes there has been a good deal of controversy. That it was far from being uniformly a period of stagnation has been particularly emphasized by recent commentators: that judged by production indices and technical advance it was in fact the contrary, and that for wage-earners who retained their employment it was a period of economic gain rather than of loss.[2] But the fact that it was a period of gathering economic crisis, in the sense of a sharpening conflict between growth of productive power and of business profitability, has not been seriously denied; and all the signs suggest that, in the case of British Capitalism at least, certain quite fundamental changes in the economic situation were occurring in this last quarter of the nineteenth century.

In our estimate of its significance much necessarily depends upon our diagnosis; . . . . For example, how far, if at all, could the economic *malaise* of the '70's be attributed to a partial saturation of investment opportunities . . . —to a fall in the rate of profit due to the rapidity of capital accumulation as such, which had gone ahead of the possibilities of augmenting the mass of surplus-value capable of being extracted from the process of production, even if the demand for commodities had expanded *pari passu* with production and no serious limitation of markets had emerged? Or how far was it due to the failure of effective demand to keep pace with the expansion of production—to a waning influence of those buoyancy-factors of which we have spoken; and in particular to the failure of consumption to expand *pari passu* with the expansion of productive power directed towards the output of consumption goods?

There is probably some evidence of the existence of the first type of situation in the fact that the real wages of labour were rising in the middle decades of the century; since this could be taken as a *prima facie* indication of the fact that demand for labour was beginning to outrun the expansion of the proletarian army, and that the situation which the

---

[1] Preface to 2nd Edition of *The Condition of the Working Class in England.*

[2] A fact which, incidentally, does much to explain the stubborn opposition at the time of the so-called "Old Unionism" to the militant tendencies of the "New Unionism", leading to a rift in the ranks of Labour; just as a somewhat parallel phenomenon (as we shall see below) goes to explain the strong survival of an "aristocracy of labour" tradition in the British Labour movement in the 1920's and the '30's.

Ricardians had feared was coming to pass. According to Professor Bowley's estimates, money-wages rose from 58 in 1860 (1914 = 100) to 80 by 1874, and real wages from 51 to 70. Most significant for investment, building labour costs are estimated to have risen between 1860 and 1875 by nearly 50 per cent., and much faster than the cost of prime materials. To this rise of wages the growing organization of skilled labour as a result of the national amalgamated unions of the '50's and '60's no doubt contributed. The 1860's were a period of abnormally rapid capital investment and of very great expansion of the productive equipment of industry. For example, between 1866 and 1872 the world output of pig-iron had increased from 8.9 million tons to 14.4 million, of which increase Great Britain had been responsible for two-fifths. In the Cleveland district about thirty new blast-furnaces had been built between 1869 and 1874 alone, increasing the productive power of this area by 50 per cent. In the hæmatite area of Cumberland and North Lancashire there was an expansion of about 25 per cent. in the early years of the '70's, and Lincolnshire in four years increased its furnaces for utilizing phosphoric ores from 7 to 21. Altogether the capital invested in iron works is estimated to have trebled, and in mines to have doubled between 1867 and 1875.

Moreover, in the two years which immediately preceded the crisis there was a particularly sharp rise of wages, and the unemployment figure (according to the incomplete data of the time) in 1873 was down to scarcely more than 1 per cent. Interest rates throughout the '70's were exceptionally low. Discount rates, in particular, in the winter of 1871 were (according to The Economist) "far below the level" at which they could have been expected to stand in view of the expansion of trade: a phenomenon which Alfred Marshall attributed to the fact that "the amount of capital seeking investment has been increasing so fast that, in spite of a great widening of the field of investment, it has forced down the rate of discount". Technical change had been rapid, absorbing a larger quantity of capital to set a given amount of labour in motion; but despite this, the absorption of labour into production (about the size of which no reliable statistics are available) must have proceeded at a very considerable rate.

There is a great deal to be said for the view, expressed by some contemporary writers on the Depression, that the fall of prices in the '70's and '80's, on the contrary to being occasioned by monetary influences connected with the supply of gold, as economists have so widely held, was the natural consequence of the fall in costs which the technical changes of the past few years had brought about. D. A. Wells, writing in the late '80's and speaking both of U.S.A. and of Britain, estimated that the saving in time and effort involved in production in recent years had amounted to as much as 70 or 80 per cent. "in a few" industries, "in not a few" to more than 50 per cent. and between one-third and two-fifths as a minimum average for production as a whole. It is possible that over manufacturing industry in general in this country the real cost in labour of producing commodities fell by 40 per cent. between 1850 and 1880. At any rate, there seems to be sufficient evidence that this fall of prices was not of *itself* a sign of sagging demand. On the other hand, if the fall in price was wholly to be interpreted in terms of technical improvement and fall in costs, the ensuing fall in profit and mood of depression remain unexplained.

Among the proximate causes of the crisis of 1873 events in the foreign investment-market are usually assigned a leading place; and it has to be remembered that prior to that date foreign investment provided an important safety-valve against any tendency of the process of accumulation to outdistance the possibilities of profitable employment at home. This foreign investment was modest compared with the dimensions which it later assumed, and was by no means an unfailing device, as events were to show. But it was far from being a negligible factor. The immediate onset of the crisis was associated with an abrupt closing of this safety-valve. Between 1867 and 1873 there had been a series of loans to Egypt, to Russia, to Hungary, to Peru, to Chile, to Brazil, together with a number of special railway loans, in addition to numerous distinctly shady ventures. Of the two milliard dollars of American railway capital floated between 1867 and 1873 British capitalists subscribed a very substantial part. "The favourite business for many years before 1873", said Sir Robert Giffen, "had become that of foreign investment". The bankruptcy of Spain and the nonpayment of interest on the Turkish debt were douches of cold water to the prevailing investment mood; and financial difficulties in countries "more or less farmed by the capital of England and other old countries (as Giffen put it), such as Austria and later South America ("almost a domain of England") and Russia, caused an abrupt paralysis of the market for foreign loans.

After an initial check to investment, the result was to encourage increased investment in the home market instead. This fact served to explain one of the most curious features of the depression: the extent to which production and productive capacity continued to increase at a pace only slightly moderated as compared with the decade before 1870. This expansion of productive capacity was specially marked in the capital goods industries during the middle '70's. The number of blast-furnaces continued to grow; and capital goods production as a whole rose from an index figure of 55.3 in 1873 to 61.6 in 1877. At the end of 1877 home investment also collapsed, as foreign investment had done some years before. But despite this, the index of capital goods production was only eight points lower in 1879 than it had been in 1877; and despite an unemployment figure of over 10 per cent. the production index had only fallen between 1873 and 1879 from 62 to 60. A revival of home investment contributed to the short-lived recovery of 1880–83. But the continuing increase of productive capacity in this period, piled upon the expansion before 1873, served to exert a further downward pressure on prices and on profit-margins in the middle '80's; and as Goschen remarked in 1885, "capitalists find it exceedingly difficult to find a good return for their capital". Over a decade the price of iron fell by 60 per cent. or even more, and the price of coal by over 40 per cent. Steel which sold for £12 in 1874 was selling for only £4 5s. in 1884. Much of this fall, as we have seen, was to be explained as a result of economies of cost due to technical improvement. . . . To a small, but only minor, extent can the price-changes be attributed to a fall in money-wages, which fell by rather less than 10 per cent. between their peak in 1874 and 1880, after which they remained more or less stationary, or even rose slightly. But it seems clear that the fall in price, consequent on the increased productive capacity, must in most directions have exceeded what could be explained in terms of cost-reduction alone. According to Sir Lothian Bell's evidence before the Royal Commission on the Depression of Trade and Industry, the production of pig-iron in the world at large had swollen by the impressive figure of 82 per cent. between 1870 and 1884, and British production alone by 31 per cent.; which had contributed to "a very considerable decline in price", exceeding any compensating decline in costs, with the consequence (the witness added, no doubt with the exaggeration to which industrialists are prone on such occasions) that "workmen were getting all the profit and iron manufacturers none". The Commission in their Final Report found that similar conditions prevailed in coal, while in textiles "profits have been much reduced" in face of production which "had been maintained or increased". The general conclusion they reached regarding industry and trade as a whole was expressed as follows: "We think that . . . over-production has been one of the most prominent features of the course of trade during recent years; and that the depression under which we are now suffering may be partially explained by this fact. . . . The remarkable feature of the present situation, and that which in our opinion distinguishes it from all previous periods of depression, is the length of time during which this over-production has continued. . . . We are satisfied that in recent years, and more particularly in the years during which the depression of trade has prevailed, the production of commodities generally and the accumulation of capital in this country have been proceeding at a rate more rapid than the increase of population". A recent commentator has given this interpretation to the "over-production" aspect of the Great Depression: "Output was expanding, the supply of men was limited. Capital was not sufficiently a substitute for labour. Although labour-saving machinery might be introduced, its results for industry as a whole were not on a scale large enough to reduce the demand for labour so sharply as to permit a reduction in money-wages".[3]

When we turn to consider the influence of the market-factor, evidence of its contribution is rather clearer, and indications are fairly plentiful that those "buoyancy-factors" which had sustained demand earlier in the century were slackening, or at least were failing to grow in influence as the immense expansion of productive capacity demanded if it was to be fully utilized. True, the stimulus of invention seemed to continue unabated; and the rate of obsolescence of machinery (involving a greater consequential demand over the period of, say, a decade for equipment in replacement) was probably accelerated (save for a few exceptions) rather than retarded. To this the Bessemer process in steel, the turbine and improved marine engines, hydraulic machinery and machine tools (the latter largely as the result of improved precision-gauges and the spread of the custom of working to gauge), the introduction of steel rollers in flour-making, of the Siemens "tank-furnace" in glass-making, of sewing machines and the rotary press are all witnesses. Even so, there is a good deal of reason for supposing that the *proportional* effect that these innovations exerted on the market for capital goods was considerably less powerful than the influence of the inventions of the first half of the century had been on the much smaller capital goods industry of the time. Railway building, which had constituted such a powerful stimulus in the middle of the century, was tapering off, at least; even though one cannot say, in face of the revival of railway construction in the later '80's and its spread to Africa and Asia, that it had yet reached saturation. Over the seven years prior to the crisis, the total length of railways in the U.S.A. had been doubled,

[3] W. W. Rostow, "Investment and Real Wages, 1873-86," *Economic History Review*, IX (1939), 150. [The interested reader may also want to consult the essays in Rostow's *British Economy of the Nineteenth Century* (Oxford, 1948).]

and during the last four years of these seven America had built some 25,000 miles. After 1873 there was an abrupt freezing of construction projects; and this sudden decline, which accompanied the financial crisis of 1873 and 1874, was a potent immediate cause of the break. Moreover, the substitution of steel rails for iron, with their greater longevity, was at the same time causing an appreciable economy in the replacement-demand for metal which a given length of existing track created.

Of particular importance for British industry was the sharp contraction of the export demand, which was only partly a consequence of the decline of foreign investment and of the cessation of railway-construction orders. In the years immediately preceding 1873 British exports had undergone a very great expansion in quantity and even more in value. Between 1867 and 1873 our foreign trade had risen by more than a third, and by 1873 total exports were 80 per cent. larger than they had been in 1860. The increase in export of iron and steel was even more remarkable: a growth of 66 per cent. between 1868 and 1872 alone. Then came the turn of the tide, unexpected and alarming. By 1876 exports of British produce had shrunk (in value) by 25 per cent. compared with the peak of 1872. Exports to the U.S.A. alone were halved, and exports of iron and steel receded by one-third in tonnage and by more than 40 per cent. in values. The collapse of the rail-iron market was specially severe. And although American railroad construction showed a cautious recovery in 1878, and there were bursts of activity again in 1882 and 1887, an increasing proportion of American railway-equipment was supplied, after the early '70's, from her own growing iron and steel industry. Never in previous depressions, as Sir Robert Giffen explained, had Britain's export trade shrunk so drastically. Despite recoveries in the export figure in 1880 and again in 1890, it was not until the turn of the century that the peak-figure (in values) of 1872–73 was surpassed. . . .

If there may be some obscurity about the causation of the Great Depression, there is much less about its effects on British Capitalism. Having witnessed the drastic effect of competition in cutting prices and profit-margins, business-men showed increasing fondness for measures whereby competition could be restricted, such as the protected or privileged market and the price and output agreement. This enhanced concern with the dangers of unrestrained competition came at a time when the growing concentration of production, especially in heavy industry, was laying the foundation for greater centralization of ownership and of control of business policy. In the newer industry of Germany and the United States this centralization was to be earlier on the scene than in Britain, where the structure of business, with its foundations firmly laid in the first part of the century, had developed according to a more individualist pattern, and the tradition attaching to this structure was more stubborn in survival. In the structure of economic as of human organisms ageing bones are apt to grow rigid. In America the '70's saw the rise of the trusts, which had sufficiently grown in extent and structure to provoke the legislation against trust companies in the late '80's and the more sweeping Sherman Act of 1890 directed against "combination in restraint of trade". In Germany associations of producers in the iron industry and the coal industry were formed in the '70's, and over the next three decades multiplied in these and other industries, until in 1905 there were stated (by the Kartell-Commission of that year) to be something in the neighbourhood of 400 cartels: a development which, in the words of Liefmann, a well-known apologist for cartels, was "a product . . . of the entire modern development of industry, with its increasing competition, the increasing risks of capital and the falling profit".[4] In England stable forms of price-agreement probably did not assume considerable dimensions until the opening of the new century, and even in iron and steel the beginnings of the amalgamation movement (which was on a more modest scale than in America) date from the late '90's. But it is significant that the International Rail-makers' Agreement (for partitioning the export-market), in which British producers participated, and the start of the "fair trade" agitation, with its plea for restricting the intrusion of "dumped" foreign products into the home market, both date from the '80's. The depression of the last quarter of the century in England was relatively little marked by the extensive excess capacity which was to become so prominent a feature of the second Great Depression of the inter-war period: it was essentially a depression of cut-throat competition and cut-prices of the classic textbook type. A leading difference between the events of the earlier and the later period, which in so many other respects provoke comparison, is that in the interval the monopolistic policy of meeting a shrinkage of demand by output-restriction and price-maintenance had come to prevail. We have earlier quoted Professor Heckscher's characterization of the mercantilist epoch of earlier centuries as obsessed by the "fear of goods". The new period that was now dawning, and which already in the '80's was being spoken of as

---

[4] Cit. C. Dawson, *Evolution of Modern Germany* (London, 1908), 174. Cf. also H. Levy, *Industrial Germany* (Cambridge, 1935), 2–18. By 1925 the number of German cartels was said to be about 3,000.

one of neo-Mercantilism, was to be increasingly obsessed with a similar fear: a fear which from one of goods was to become a fear of productive capacity.

The last two decades of the nineteenth century were also marked by another preoccupation which recalled the Mercantilism of earlier centuries: a preoccupation with privileged spheres of foreign trade. Closely joined with this went an interest in privileged spheres of foreign investment. This concern with foreign investment was a distinctive mark of the new period, having no close likeness in its prototype. The difference marked the contrast between an age of undeveloped capital accumulation and the latter days of industrial Capitalism. Of this mature Capitalism, impelled by the need to find new extensions of the investment-field, export of capital and of capital goods constituted a leading feature. In the '80's there awakened a new-found sense of the economic value of colonies: an awakening which occurred with remarkable simultaneity among the three leading industrial Powers of Europe. . . . Business interests in centres like Birmingham and Sheffield began to raise the demand that "to make good the loss of the American market we ought to have the colonial market": and Joseph Chamberlain was to call on the Government to give protection to markets at home while taking steps to "create new markets" abroad, and to raise his glass in simultaneous toast of "Commerce and Empire, because, gentlemen, the Empire, to parody a celebrated expression, is Commerce".[5] In similar vein, writers in Germany at the turn of the century were talking of the participation of Germany "in the policy of expansion out of Europe, at first modestly, of late with growing decision", as being compelled by "the enormous increase of its industrial production and its trade", and of German activities in the Near East as "doing what we are doing in other parts of the world—seeking new markets for our exports and new spheres of investment for our capital". . . .

The Great Depression, whose course we have traced in England, by no means confined its attentions to this country. Its incidence was

[5] Speech to the Congress of the Chambers of Commerce of the Empire, London, June 10, 1896; also speech at Birmingham, June 22, 1894; cit. L. Woolf, *Empire and Commerce in Africa: A Study in Economic Imperialism* (London, 1919), 18. In the latter speech he declared that he "would never lose the hold we now have over our great Indian dependency—by far the greatest and most valuable of all the customers we have". "For the same reason [i.e. need for creating markets] I approve of the continued occupation of Egypt; and for the same reason I have urged upon this Government . . . the necessity for using every legitimate opportunity to extend our influence and control in that great African continent which is now being opened up to civilization and commerce."

heavy alike in Germany, in Russia, and in the U.S.A.; although France, less deeply industrialized, felt its effects more lightly and pursued a smoother course. In fact, in Germany the initial shock was more violent than it was here; and between 1873 and 1877 German iron consumption fell by as much as 50 per cent. The outcome of the depression, however, in these other countries followed somewhat different paths. In Russia the nascent factory Capitalism of the late '60's and early '70's received a sharp setback from the crisis of the middle '70's: a depression which was prolonged for ten to fifteen years. But the early '90's witnessed a quick recovery, stimulated by a renewed burst of railway building, and in the investment boom that followed the number of factory workers increased by a half and the production of factory industry doubled. In Germany there were elements of buoyancy which brought revival sooner than elsewhere and gave it more strength when it came. For one thing, the industrial revolution had only recently begun, and until the unification of Germany had been restricted in scope. The events of 1866–1872 proved to be a crucial turning-point in her economic development. The last three decades of the century were to witness a rapid urbanization of Germany; and the population showed a higher annual average increase during the second half than it had in the first half of the century. The growth of the electrical industry and to a less extent of the chemical industry also played an important rôle in stimulating revival, especially in the later '90's. In the U.S.A. the "expanding frontier", with its rich possibilities for both investment and markets, and a labour-reserve swelled by immigration as well as by a large natural increase of population, gave to American Capitalism in the last quarter of the nineteenth century a resilience which the older Capitalism of Great Britain could not have. . . .

In England, there can be small doubt that it was the revival of capital export and the opportunities which the new Imperialism afforded which was the essential factor in that new phase of prosperity between 1896 and 1914. This Indian summer caused memories of the Great Depression to fade out of mind. It rehabilitated the reputation of Free Trade, grown tarnished during the depression years. It brought renewed faith in the destiny of Capitalism to make economic progress eternal. Socialism was to be heard again as a street-gospel in the 1890's and the 1900's; while the Labour Party was to grow to be a political force after 1906. But the belief in Capitalism as a working system was not in England seriously shaken in the decade prior to the first Great War.

THE POSTWAR ADVANCE OF THE FIVE HUNDRED MILLION *

Max Ways †

. . . .

The great underappreciated fact in the world today is the magnitude of the advanced countries' forward surge in the two decades, now nearly completed, since World War II ended. This surge is all the more significant because it followed upon a long period when capitalism seemed to have lost its thrust. In the interwar decades many people came to believe that if the world ever saw another forward surge comparable to that preceding 1914, the progress would come through socialism and much of it would be made in the backward countries then trying to cast off imperial yokes. The postwar role of the vanguard countries, in this view, was to mark time while waiting for the parade to catch up.

Instead, the advanced countries leaped forward, adding more to their total product in less than twenty years than they had added in the preceding fifty. Within each of the advanced countries there was some degree of postwar liberalization from the state's intervention in capitalist processes, an intervention that had been growing before and during the war; there was a very marked liberalization in international trade among the advanced countries. As a result, competition flourished after 1945, and in the allocation of resources the role of national and international markets waxed.

One unexpected and unwanted result was a postwar widening of the gap between the advanced countries and the underdeveloped—a widening that occurred in spite of the dissolution of empires and the substantial assistance extended by the advanced countries to those lagging behind. By 1964, answers to the moral, political, and economic

* Reprinted from *Fortune,* August 1964, pp. 104–9, 212–14. Courtesy of *Fortune* magazine.

† Max Ways is a journalist of many years' experience, Assistant Managing Editor of *Fortune* magazine, and the author of *Beyond Survival,* an essay on the place, aims, and prospects of the United States in the postwar world.

problems arising from sharp disparities in levels of living did not seem so quick and easy as they had looked in 1945. But the astounding postwar advance of the advanced, by cutting the ground from under the unfruitful socialist and statist premises that had gained credence in the stagnant prewar years, had laid a firmer foundation for progress in *all* the free nations. By 1964 it was beginning to be apparent that the advanced countries depended for their success upon something other than imperial power or physical resources or machines; that these assets were, in fact, the products of individual attitudes and social institutions which could be copied, assimilated, and modified by the underdeveloped countries, but which could not be seized or accepted as packaged gifts—or successfully bypassed. In this sense, the postwar achievement of the advanced countries—if it is understood—may turn out to be of immense long-range benefit to the underdeveloped countries. But there is little chance that the underdeveloped countries will grasp the lesson of the postwar decades unless the peoples of the advanced countries themselves come to have a keener appreciation of the size and meaning of their own achievement.

The meaning of these figures is often obscured by a deadly phrase —"of course." In retrospect, we regard it as "inevitable" that the industrial production of the seven leading countries should have doubled in sixteen years. "Naturally," this was done while the average length of the work week was being reduced. "Of course," at the same time the seven countries increased agricultural production by nearly 50 percent. "Of course," they managed to provide more goods and services per capita for an increased population, and at the same time expanded the capital plant that will build tomorrow's goods. "Of course," in the U.S. the existing stock of plant and equipment rose nearly 70 percent from 1947 to 1963.

The smug "of course" with which capitalist nations tend to ignore the record of their past achievements is rarely matched by any complacency about the present or future. A system that depends at bottom upon narrowly calculated risks, a system committed to expansion and vulnerable to any falling behind, is bound to concentrate attention on its "problems." In the U.S. any mention of the great postwar economic achievement is drowned in the tremendous volume of discussion about the persistence of poverty, about unemployment, about the threat of automation.

In times of prosperity like the present, the fear of a downturn always stalks the land. The business cycle absorbs the attention of a high proportion of all the sophisticated effort devoted to economic analysis and prediction. It could hardly be otherwise. Individual firms can suffer grave damage—or miss rich opportunities—if their decisions are ill timed in relation to the business cycle. Within a whole national or international economy deep or frequent business recessions can so multiply anxieties and resentments that political repercussions will plunge capitalism into the fundamental risk (to be discussed presently) that political controls will impair its ability to function. So the continuing concern over cycles is justified.

Time out from Knuckle Gnawing

Yet it is also true that the effect of recessions on the long-range curve of production is greatly exaggerated in public mythology. [On a chart of] industrial production in seven [leading] countries [U.S., Canada, U.K., France, West Germany, Italy, Japan] over a fifteen-year span, there is only one year—1958—when the index falls back to the level of two years before. Even the great depression was not a return to the Stone Age; at the nadir of 1933 the U.S. gross national product did not fall below that of the prosperous year 1920—and per capita U.S. income was only a shade below that of 1915. In none of the advanced countries has the material condition of any large part of the population failed to exhibit in any peacetime year of the twentieth century a distinct improvement over the conditions of the preceding generation. The phrase "three generations from shirtsleeves to shirtsleeves" no longer represents reality in the advanced countries—if, indeed, it ever did. A very small proportion of all families that lift their levels of income and education ever sink back.

One of capitalism's numerous paradoxes lies in this: the market economy is *both* a highly resilient system with a powerful forward thrust and also a system that would not be secure if it did not generate anxieties and "trepidation." The postwar advance, however, is so huge and so significant that the universal knuckle gnawing should be interrupted from time to time for an appreciative look around at what is going on.

.   .   .   .

The Buffalo Breed Faster

There is some interesting knuckle gnawing over growth rates in a recent book that has attracted considerable attention, Angus Maddison's

Economic Growth in the West. The title, however, does not express the author's interest nearly so precisely as his subtitle: *Comparative Experience in Europe and North America.* He is dealing with the postwar period, but he takes for granted the huge expansion that the advanced nations have in common, concentrating instead upon what he regards as a more intriguing question: Why do the advanced nations on the European continent show faster growth rates than Great Britain, Canada, and the U.S.? In answering, he gives much praise to more skillful and more vigorously expansionist governmental and central-bank policies pursued on the Continent. But he suggests other answers, too, and some of these may have a more general lesson. On the Continent "the liberalization of trade has so far been a very positive stimulus to high growth of demand and better allocation of resources." Madison expects that for several decades to come European growth rates will be "much higher than the long-run historical experience" mainly because "the productivity level in Europe is only half that in the U.S., and most of this productivity gap is due to missed investment opportunities. The European countries are working below the fringe of best-practice technology . . . They benefit from the fact that they will be harnessing techniques and factor combinations which to a wide degree are already known. The U.S., having borne these pioneering burdens in the field of technology, has more restricted opportunities for productivity growth." Maddison does not assert that the U.S., because it is the leader, is permanently doomed to slower growth rates; only that the European countries have a chance to close a gap created by their relatively slow prewar growth.

Nobody can say what future growth rates in the advanced countries will or "ought to" be. Probably the other six countries, as they approach the present level of U.S. per capita income, will follow the U.S. in devoting a larger proportion of their total effort to "services." For many decades productivity gains in the services sector have been much lower than in agriculture and manufacturing. From this, some might conclude that future growth rates in the advanced countries as a group will probably be lower than they have been. But that would be an incautious calculation. For all we know, in the years ahead services will develop a much more lively rate of productivity increase. Even if this does not happen, we cannot know that the future productivity rates in manufacturing and agriculture will not advance even more rapidly than they have. World use of commercial fertilizers, for example, has quadrupled in eighteen years, most of the increase being in the advanced countries, none of which is approaching technological saturation in fertilizer use. Similarly, the "threat of automation" is in its long-range significance a promise of higher industrial productivity rates.

But all such crystal gazing, interesting and important as it is in certain contexts, pales to insignificance alongside the great rediscovery of the postwar period: capitalism as a whole is *not* subject to a ceiling of diminishing returns; innovation is *not* a self-exhausting process; the era of radical change we now experience is *not* headed toward a new "point of rest"; all the buffalo of opportunity on the plains of progress have *not* been shot—indeed, they are breeding faster and faster.

This rediscovery, dwarfing all the endemic anxieties and problems of capitalism, may turn out to be one of the decisive turns of the twentieth century. This reversal of expectations is by no means complete; the political rhetoric of all the advanced countries is still heavily (though decreasingly) loaded with the old, discouraged assumptions of the interwar period (for a well-preserved example of which see Walter Reuther's statement opening the 1964 automobile labor negotiations). Nevertheless, the reversal of expectations ought to be recognized as a dominating feature of the postwar landscape.

The Years of Stagnation

The significance of the revived confidence in capitalism can be seen when the interwar period is placed in a historical perspective. The stagnant period that began for many advanced nations soon after World War I (although it did not reach the U.S. until a decade later) was the first really major setback in the progressive development of the capitalist world, a development that had been running in some countries for at least two hundred years. Historical interpretation used to fix the industrial revolution, which began in England in the late eighteenth century, as the dividing line. This view is being replaced by interpretations that stress the enterprising state of mind, rather than the machine, as the determinative factor of the new age. This state of mind was quite apparently spreading for at least three generations before the new spirit found its mechanized servants. The machines multiplied rapidly, but the enterprising attitude implied such a deep departure from the past that it was bound to spread slowly and often painfully.

. . . .

Looking back, 1914 can be seen as a political breakdown of the external relations among national states, though at the time and for a generation thereafter "capitalist rivalry" got most of the blame for the war. Nationalism, even in its catastrophe, was disclosed as a far more powerful force than had been supposed. Its ability to conscript men and machines and call forth unprecedented and sustained sacrifice was a fact that overshadowed the imaginations of the post-1918 world. The war's damage to international business was never repaired and as economic trouble developed, first in Europe, later in the U.S., each national state in its newly displayed power was expected to "mobilize the national resources" or "fight the depression as we fought the war." The old relationship between government and the enterprise system changed from one in which the states were supposed to provide the national and international legal framework that the economic system needed, to one in which each national government came to be regarded as holding the prime responsibility for economic progress and well-being. The socialist tendencies that spread in the interwar period owed as much to Kaiser Wilhelm as to his more famous countryman, Karl Marx.

Even in those nations that preserved their democracy there were strong pressures for a return to the halfway house of mercantilism. In the 1930's international trade was less and less free and was conducted with increasing overtones of nationalist economic warfare. All the advanced countries adopted internal political programs intended to "correct" the operation of capitalist markets. Equalization of incomes was sought through progressive taxation. Business was heavily and often clumsily regulated. As the capitalist machine faltered under these burdens, its flagging pace generated demands for more and more government intervention. Sluggish production and investment figures seemed to confirm the theoretical conclusion that capitalism had outlived its vigor.

"Geared to Incessant Economic Change"

The wonder is that World War II did not deepen this belief to the point where political restraints upon capitalism would have extinguished its chance of survival. This was indeed the gloomy expectation of many men whose own preference was for the success of capitalism. An interesting view of the postwar prospect is contained in an essay, "Capitalism in the Postwar World," by the distinguished Harvard economist, Joseph A. Schumpeter, published in 1943. "It is a commonplace that capitalist society is, and for some time has been, in a state of decay," he wrote. "But there is no agreement about the precise nature of that decay." He set up two theories to explain the decay. He did not agree with the theory of vanishing investment opportunity, of which the outstanding exponent was Alvin H. Hansen. Schumpeter began his characterization of Hansen's theory in a memorable passage: "It starts from an undeniable truth, more or less explicit recognition of which constitutes its chief merit. Unlike other economic systems, the capitalist system is geared to incessant economic change. Its very nature implies recurrent industrial revolutions which are the main sources of the profit and interest incomes of entrepreneurs and capitalists and supply the main opportunities for new investments—such as railroad building or the construction of electric-power plants—and the main outlets for new savings. Whereas a stationary feudal economy would still be a feudal economy, and a stationary socialist economy would still be a socialist economy, stationary capitalism is a contradiction in terms . . . Its most characteristic types, processes and institutions all become atrophic in a stationary world."

While agreeing with this major premise of the vanishing-investment-opportunity theory, Schumpeter did not accept the minor premise, that capitalism had in fact then reached a point where it was bound to stagnate because no great innovations were in sight, no new lands were available for development, and the birthrate was falling. On purely economic grounds Schumpeter thought capitalism's expansion could continue indefinitely.

His own theory of the decay of capitalism introduced social and political elements. He noted that all the stultifying factors mentioned in Hansen's theory reduced profit expectations. But there was a more obvious and direct cause of the weakening of profit expectations—"the anticapitalist policies adopted, in most European countries, ever since the first world war and, in the U.S., since 1933." Schumpeter expected these anticapitalist policies to be extended in the postwar period because capitalism changes society in such a way that the voters turn against it. For instance, it destroys "the old aristocracies who knew so much better how to rule than does the businessman." (Schumpeter grew up in Vienna where this view was well established.) It destroys the independent farmers, the artisans, and small traders "who count at the polls." He expected (correctly) that the majority of "the intellectuals" would oppose the revival of capitalism in the postwar world. Against this background of diminishing political support, Schumpeter examined the almost universal expectation that a postwar slump was bound to occur. He believed capitalism had the inherent capacity to surmount this danger, but that—politically—it would not be given a chance to do so. The very expectation of a postwar slump would encourage such anticapitalist policies as the indefinite continuance of wartime controls over prices and wages and the prewar tax policies that aimed at the redistribution of wealth. He expected a postwar period of "capitalism in the oxygen tent," kept alive by public expenditure "as a permanent device of regulating the pulse of the nation's economic life." Such a system would work so badly that it would become "perfectly natural—in fact it may be a practical necessity—to take further steps toward state management," i.e., toward socialism.

In 1964, with profits healthy, with innovation moving at a faster pace than ever before, with most of the globe yearning desperately to join the march of economic expansion, with populations rising everywhere, it is easy to smile at Hansen's belief that capitalism would decay because investment opportunities were vanishing. But even now Schumpeter's view of capitalism's peril is no smiling matter. Although his prediction was wrong in the short run, the anticapitalist political tendencies he describes represent a permanent or, at least, a very durable hazard to capitalism. Because the danger, in one form or another, is likely to recur, the question of how the danger came to be surmounted in the immediate postwar period is of more than historical interest.

An Undercurrent Begins to Run

Probably the deepest influence in reducing anticapitalist pressures was a lesson implicit in the war itself. The evil (and then the failure) of totalitarian governments revived in the public mind certain old reservations about unlimited government. Suddenly, there was an audience for that minority of the intellectuals who had been warning against turning always to government for relief from capitalism's anxieties and disturbances. With concrete examples before the world's horrified eyes, such a book as Friedrich Hayek's *The Road to Serfdom* was taken seriously in the middle Forties whereas before the war it would have been dismissed as mere shuddering at imaginary dangers "under the bed." This is not to say that capitalism became popular in the postwar world; it had never generated much enthusiasm, and quite possibly it never will. But a strong undercurrent began running in all the advanced nations against the pre-1945 assumption that governments would have to take over more and more of economic life.

After a struggle in every case, wartime controls over prices and wages were dismantled in country after country. Predictions that there would be no jobs for returning soldiers proved false; through the post-war period in all the advanced countries the number of people employed rose. Most of the additional goods they produced were absorbed by expanding internal markets, confounding Marxists and many others who had believed the markets of advanced countries would be "saturated," as soon as wartime shortages were made up. "The German miracle" was a demonstration of how wrong had been the Nazi dogma that the Germans could not prosper unless they had political control of land and potential markets to the east; freeing the German economy brought more material gain to West Germans than Hitler would have obtained by winning the war. Other demonstrations—"the French miracle," "the Italian miracle," "the Japanese miracle"—followed. In each case the internal national market proved expansible.

While it's true that most of the postwar economic expansion has been "national"—in the sense that most of the additional product was consumed in its country of origin—in a broader sense the key battles for a liberated and expanding economic order were fought on issues of ihternational trade. This is the strategic area because anxiety generated by capitalist disturbance from "outside" always has an especially strong emotional claim upon government intervention—and government intervention, under twentieth-century conditions, tends to work back from control over international business to control over internal business. A converse point is also true: every statist planner knows (or soon learns) that his blueprints for the domestic economy become meaningless unless he can control foreign trade and the flow of capital across his borders. Thus, in a double sense, the postwar revival of capitalism depended upon limiting the tendency of national governments to interfere with international commerce.

. . . .

To summarize, the postwar advance is based on two kinds of accumulation that are going on simultaneously: within each advanced country there is a steady "vertical" rise in the number of machines, the amount of electrical energy, and the number of skilled, educated, self-improving people; there is also a "horizontal" accumulation in the ever widening world markets.

The Turnaround in Top Policy

Neither of these would be moving at their recent pace if changes had not occurred in the climate in which profit expectations are calculated. These calculations never result in certainty because capitalism implies competition, which implies risk. As the advanced societies rise far above subsistence levels, as a larger proportion of individuals' income is diverted to objects other than the bare necessities of life, the risks increase for those who provide these "discretionary" goods and services that customers can accept or reject. A further increase of risk occurs as the pace of innovation steps up. . . . If the pre-1945 political policies that deliberately dampened profit expectations were reintroduced into the 1960's world of greater built-in risk, the consequences might be disastrous.

. . . .

This shift of basic attitude need not imply the sweeping away of all or most of the legal changes affecting business that were adopted in the interwar period. Some of these—e.g., farm price supports—are so grossly inconsistent with a market economy and so damaging to free international trade that their eventual repeal must be sought. But there are many other interwar measures—e.g., the U.S. regulation of securities markets—that can be administered in ways consistent with the revived confidence in capitalism. There is no point in pretending that the national and international legal frameworks existing in 1914 would have been adequate for all time—or even that they were adequate then. For those committed to capitalism as an economic system the appropriate public policy goal is not a simple reduction of government action affecting business; the appropriate goal is government action more consistent with the nature, the needs, and the potentialities of capitalism. Government *direction* of economic activity will become less and less fruitful as the pace of change accelerates; but capitalism will always continue to be dependent on the evolution of a strong national and international framework of business law.

Three Goals of Education

Public acceptance of capitalism or public animosity toward it and the changes it brings will depend largely upon the whole quality of life in the capitalist societies, and not merely upon the rate of material growth. Nor are the police powers of government and the economic responsibilities of corporations the only factors that determine the quality of life. The changing society requires an immense amount of public business that is done through organizations which are neither purely commercial nor purely governmental.

For instance, education, which in the U.S. is conducted by local communities and private organizations, is a decisive factor not only in the pace of economic advance but in the quality of life. Education in the advanced societies has three distinct roles, listed here in ascending order of importance:

1. Implanting the basic skills, such as genuine literacy, which will enable people to learn a succession of specific skills throughout their working lives.

2. Implanting the desire for self-improvement. Unless this quality is widespread in a modern capitalist society, it will stagnate and if it stagnates capitalism will become, as Schumpeter put it, a contradiction in terms. The hard lessons of life in a capitalist society—competition within cooperation, individual responsibility within discipline—are introduced in the classroom. Unschooled societies are economically backward not so much because their people lack specific skills as because they lack an ingrained drive for improvement. Similarly, American employers are loath to hire school dropouts not mainly because specific skills are absent but because dropouts are suspected of lacking the desire to acquire skills. If this part of their schooling did not "take" they are not yet part of the five hundred million.

3. The third and most important role of education has nothing whatever to do with increasing the pace of capitalist production. It relates to the uses, individual and social, that people decide to make of the potentialities of capitalism.

The values that determine these decisions are at bottom ethical and aesthetic. Capitalism is an economic system that vastly widens the practical field of ethical and aesthetic choice. But capitalism, as any observers of an American city will agree, contains no built-in bent toward the good or the beautiful. Failure to understand capitalism's basically limited and humble role in the totality of life causes much of the bitterness and disillusionment that is directed toward it.

. . . .

In the things that count most the advanced countries have every reason to feel discontented with their present condition. But let the blame fall where it belongs—on the master, not his servant, the capitalist economy. No bugles will ever blow for the triumphal march of the economic regime of anxiety and trepidation. Bugles might someday blow for the uses to which men may put the unparalled opportunities opened up by this regime.